PRAISE FOR SCOTT GUERIN

"The author's careful illustration of his introduction to religion, description of his devout faith that was punctuated by nagging questions, his approach to seeking the answers, and his interpretation of his findings are a refreshing account of a journey that offers numerous perspectives along the way. **A highly recommended read that demonstrates how curiosity and the questioning of traditional thinking can illuminate many different paths** to exploring an individual's spiritual journey."
— Jill Cantelmo, PhD

"If you have ever pondered the seemingly endless questions about God, religion, or spirituality, this book will get you thinking. **The author examines myriad religious/spiritual uncertainties and conundrums**, inevitably ones you have wrestled with yourself."
— Mark Vogel, PhD

"Life is a journey, and **you come away from reading this book feeling confident** in all its twists and turns. Anyone who questions their faith, or struggles to accept the religious beliefs of their parents will find comfort in this intimate story."
— Maureen Saks

"The author takes us along his own heartfelt journey and explains how he became open and enlightened spiritually. **He also uses a more scientific approach to back up his spiritual beliefs**. I would highly recommend this book to anyone who struggles with the rigidity and exclusive nature of traditional religions."
— Amazon Reviewer

"I thoroughly enjoyed Dr. Guerin's account of his journey, starting from his boyhood Lutheran upbringing, through an evangelical Christian phase as a teenager and young adult, to a more spiritual approach as an older adult. The account effectively weaves the author's scholarly research into an easy-to-read and interesting personal narrative. **I finished the book anxious to learn more.**"
— Amazon Reviewer

12 LESSONS

ANGEL IN TRAINING

SCOTT GUERIN

For more information, visit Angelintraining.org

Copyright ©2020 Scott A. Guerin

ISBN: 978-0-578-69308-8

Logo developed by Jeremy Mayes
jeremy@amayes.me

Cover Design by DigiWriting

Printed and bound in Canada.

The author greatly appreciates you taking the time to read this work. Please consider leaving a review wherever you bought the book, or telling your friends or blog readers about *12 Lessons* to help spread the word. Thank you for your support.

12 Lessons. Copyright © 2020 by Scott A. Guerin. All rights reserved under International and Pan-American Copyright Conventions. This book is sold subject to the condition that it shall not, by way of trade or otherwise, be lent, re-sold, hired out, or otherwise circulated without the publisher's prior consent in any form of binding or cover other than that in which it is published and without a similar condition including this condition being imposed on the subsequent purchaser.

CONTENTS

Praise for Scott Guerin 1

Acknowledgments 9

Where Are You? How Did You Get Here? 13

LESSON 1:
We Create Our Perceptions about God 17

LESSON 2:
Religion and Spirituality Are Two Distinct Concepts 27

LESSON 3:
There Are Many Ways to God 35

LESSON 4:
Resolving Conflicting Beliefs 47

LESSON 5:
Who Decides What Is True? 55

Prayer: A Lifeline? 63

Does Praying for Others Work? 69

LESSON 6:
Meditation Is an Effective Way to Experience Peace and the Presence of God 77

LESSON 7:
God Is Still Communicating 87

LESSON 8:
There Is No Separation between God and Us 103

LESSON 9:
Validating Belief Systems 111

LESSON 10:
We Are All Angels 121

LESSON 11:
The Law of Attraction 129

How the Law of Attraction Works 139

Three Experiments with the Law of Attraction 153

LESSON 12:
We Are Cocreators of Our Reality 161

On Being Angels 175

COMING SOON!
Angel in Training – Calling all Angels! 183

Suggested Readings 184

References 186

To Mom, who embedded in me the thirst for research that has propelled me throughout my life, and to Dad who showed me how to be kind and courageous.

Lew and Flora Guerin both passed in the spring of 2020 from complications as a result of COVID-19. Miss you both beyond words.

OTHER BOOKS BY SCOTT GUERIN

Other books in the Angel in Training Series by Scott Guerin

Angel in Training
12 Lessons: A Path Forward
Calling All Angels!

ACKNOWLEDGMENTS

Thank you to all of you who have supported the first iteration of this idea in *Angel in Training: A Spiritual Journey*. Your notes, messages, and discussions were greatly appreciated and sparked the idea of expanding on the lessons introduced in the book. A special thanks to Steve Wickes, a friend of over fifty years, who offered to apply his analytic mind and heartfelt in-depth review of the idea of *12 Lessons*. Steve provided valuable input and, as anyone that knows him would agree, he is one of those few good men presently walking on this planet. And of course I am deeply grateful to my wife Debbie, who puts up with me and supports me like no other ever has. Love you bb.

An essential point for everyone reading these pages is that these ideas are presented as a result of my spiritual and religious journey and the many twists and turns it has taken. As you will see, I offer the lessons in the context of topics to think about and explore for yourself and are not prescriptive in any way. The bottom line is that if you are satisfied with your current beliefs, religion, or practices, *please* do not make any changes. This life is about you and your happiness.

Whether you have always wondered about certain aspects of your faith, are ready to make a change, or are excited to learn new ways to navigate this life outside of religion, these discussions will hopefully help you on your way.

ANGELS

In many religions, angels are considered spiritual beings, agents, or messengers of God. The word comes from the Greek *agnelos*, meaning messenger. In Islam, belief in angels is one of the Six Articles of Faith. Devas and dharma protectors are types of angelic beings in Buddhism and Hinduism. Other religions believe each person has a guardian angel to help them throughout life. The Judeo-Christian Bible provides detailed descriptions of angels with different powers and abilities. Interestingly, when angels are mentioned in these scriptures, they usually appear in human form.

One day, I realized we are all angels.

WHERE ARE YOU? HOW DID YOU GET HERE?

Every time I visit a new town or city, the first thing I do is find a directory displaying a map of the area. The critical component is that red dot with the label "You are here." Without that dot, the map is useless. The dot places everything into context by instantly showing me where I am in relation to where I want to go and what I want to see. This is exactly what I would like this book to be for anyone with a desire to learn more topics related to religion, spirituality, who we are, and how to navigate our lives. Whether your current faith satisfies all your needs and you are curious about other viewpoints and ideas, or if you are looking for alternatives to organized religion to continue your journey, like me, these lessons will provide some help.

These lessons grew out of my passionate life-long search to understand God and spirituality, beginning in my teenage years. When I was growing up, our family attended a Lutheran church, where I first learned about God through the lens of this Protestant religion. I participated in the worship services and classes the church offered, paying attention to every lesson and taking notes on the sermons. Then my older brother introduced us to the born-again evangelical Christian movement, and I dove in headfirst, learning all about theology, the Bible, and many aspects of the conservative Christian faith. After several years of trying to reconcile the narrow perspective of this theology with friends, classmates, and coworkers, I joined the Presbyterian church, which holds a less rigid view. I devoted many hours to teaching Sunday School classes, running the youth group, and serving on various boards. Whatever church I was involved with, I did so with everything I had.

Then it happened. Slowly, almost imperceptibly, a sadness crept into my life. As much as I wanted to shove it to the recesses of my heart and mind, it would not go away. Even more so, it got worse. Then my life crashed into the ground like a plane at full throttle. This devastation was followed by divorce, financial ruin, depression, and a night of suicidal ideation.

What the hell happened? Where was my God? Where did He go? Was He even ever there? What about all the things I did over the years? All the hours spent in prayer, working and teaching others about the love of God? I was lost.

From that point, I began to rebuild my thoughts and beliefs about God, religion, and spirituality from the ground up. Over the next thirty years, my ideas solidified into a few distinct lessons. These ideas came after years of studying psychology, specifically human and spiritual development, and the physical sciences through research in prayer, meditation, and quantum physics. As a result, I developed these *12 Lessons* as a new path forward. They do not represent a new belief system, but rather a review of fundamental topics to consider when deciding on what you choose to believe.

So that's where I am and how I got here. What about you? Where are you in your journey? Are there aspects of your faith that you have been wondering about? Do you have questions relating to the effectiveness of prayer or how we decide what we believe is true? Do you wonder if there are other sources of information available to us about God, other than ancient sacred texts? Are you curious about the Law of Attraction and how it might work? If these questions interest you, this book will help you find answers. Whether you agree with all of them or not, at the very least you will be better able to say, "I am here."

LESSON 1

WE CREATE OUR PERCEPTIONS ABOUT GOD

Our understanding of God is always expanding

After decades of passionately following my religious practice and doing everything I could to grow spiritually, I ended up in a dark place. I had passionately sought after God for decades through the churches I attended, exceeding all requirements and practices. After all that, my life was a complete disaster. At that time, I had a clear image in my mind that I was at the edge of a precipice and looking down into oblivion. It reminded me of the Nietzsche quote in the movie *Wall Street* when the young, cocky stockbroker, Bud Fox (Charlie Sheen), is arrested in his office on charges of insider trading. As the officials walk him out, his manager says to him, "When a man looks in the abyss, and nothing is staring back at him, at that moment, the man finds his character." For me, this statement meant that when my life was at a point of total devastation, with nothing left, at that point I began to see that I had substance. Something about me remained.

That something deep inside me formed firm ground. Even with no real answers to what the future held, I knew nothing could be worse than what I had just lived through. I had a sense of relief that although I had gone to the precipice and looked deep into the abyss, I had found something of myself. I felt as if I was now standing in the rubble of the burned-out building of my life. And even with what I went through, I still had a deep desire to continue my journey to understanding God and spirituality.

The first question I thought of to restart my inquiry was where and when do we learn about God and spiritual concepts? The usual suspects that come to mind include our family, religious leaders at our places of worship, and the religious texts associated with particular religious beliefs. But these are ways other people and organizations teach us about these subjects, not how we become aware of and experience God. My question was more psychological than theological, and I found out that the two do not tend to mix well.

The difference became evident when I was taking courses in Pastoral Counseling at a conservative Christian seminary I attended when I was in my twenties. In these classes, I became familiar with general psychological concepts related to the nature of human emotion, human development, and learning theories. However, one big problem, from the perspective of the conservative

Christian instructor, was that psychology approached life from a secular perspective and did not rely on the scriptures as the ultimate truth. Not too long after that, I stopped attending the seminary.

Over ten years later, I was in a much different place in my beliefs but still powerfully drawn to the subject. I was determined to go at this subject again but still skeptical about what I would learn. Throwing caution to the wind, I signed up for a few general psychology classes at a nearby university.

Throughout the coursework, I was surprised there were only a few instances where religion intersected with psychology. The main reason was that psychology and religion got off to a bad start. The founders of modern psychology unequivocally portrayed any concepts of God as nothing less than delusional. Sigmund Freud, James Skinner, and Albert Ellis stated that religion contained "wishful illusions," "universal obsessional neurosis," and even claimed that people are healthier without religion.[1] Atheists and other opponents of religion used these statements to discount beliefs about God and religion. Prominent psychologists like Carl Jung, William James, and others disagreed and presented positive views of religion and psychology.

I turned forty just after completing a master's degree, and this milestone event helped to motivate me to continue my journey. I enrolled in a doctoral program in the school of psychology at Fielding Graduate University in California. Unsure how this school approached the area of religion and spirituality, I was hesitant to declare my specific interests in spiritual development. To my surprise,

I quickly learned the faculty wholeheartedly accepted my subject of inquiry. However, they cautioned me that a scientific investigation of spirituality could be a slippery slope because religious scholars tended to interject their own biases into their research. This challenge motivated me even more, and I was excited to jump in.

In looking at ways we learn about spirituality, the discipline of human development is a good start. There are seven common human development theories we could investigate: evolutionary theory, psychosexual theory, cognitive developmental theories, theories of learning, cultural theory, social role theory, and systems theory. Books on these theories could easily fill a library.

Of these theories, for me, a system theory best describes how we learn about religious and divine concepts. System theory suggests we learn about our world as a result of our interactions between several interdependent groups called "systems." One popular system theory developed by Urie Bronfenbrenner, a Russian-born American psychologist, is called the Ecological Systems Theory.[2] It proposes that individuals develop as a result of relationships and interactions with a complex set of interconnected systems.

The system of the home is a critical time for us as we develop our ideas and impressions of God. In the weeks and months right after birth, we can sense a difference between us and our primary caregivers, usually our mothers, but do not have the ability to perceive much beyond that. Our understanding about who the others are in our systems will develop over time. When we first perceive a differences between us and others, in my opinion, is where our first impressions of God or God-like personae are formed. As we mature, we begin to gain perspective and context of who we are and how we fit in with others.

Psychologist Eric Erikson identified an important point regarding the first few months of life in his psychosocial theory of development.[2] Erikson identified eight stages of development from birth to death that most people experience. In these stages, we work through developmental tasks, as well as psychosocial crises. These crises, if not resolved in a positive way, will interfere in other stages as the child matures. I will not go into all of Erikson's stages here, but the first stage is most relevant to this discussion. According to Erikson, from birth to twenty-four months, our developmental tasks include sensory and motor development, along with communication, attachment, and emotional development. The psychosocial crisis is Trust versus Mistrust. During this time, we experience the world as a safe place if we feel availability, dependability, and sensitivity from our caregivers. Conversely, if we experience a lack of confidence in the caregiver or doubt our "lovableness," underlying doubts about the world will follow us throughout our lives. While the Trust versus Mistrust we experience is not exactly a picture of what God is like, I believe it provides a general first impression of what the world is like.

James Fowler from Emory University developed another interesting theory that sheds some light on this topic. He proposed a theory of human development that combined several stage theories for a global, unified theory called "Faith Stages."[3] Fowler drew from cognitive, social, and moral perspectives to identify how a person determines their faith system. It is important to note that Fowler's word "faith" does not necessarily mean religious beliefs, but rather a global cognitive belief system that serves as a motivating force that guides us through life. A person's faith is comprised of three general themes: centers of value, images of power, and master stories. Centers of value are a person's core concerns that are consciously or unconsciously worshiped or are powerful influences. Images of power are whatever a person believes will protect them from harm. These can take many forms, from an all-powerful God concept to an institution, government, or the size of their bank accounts. Master stories are what people tell themselves to help interpret and define events in their lives. For example, a person may tell themselves that their success and happiness are directly related to financial security as a result of achieving career goals through their abilities and efforts.

Fowler's theory, while one of many, is a good way to sum up how we learn about God and spiritual matters. As we go through our lives learning and interacting with the people in our world, we choose our core values, cling to what we think will protect us from harm, and develop a life story of who we are. All of these aspects can be based on family, cultural, social, and religious influences.

The end result of who you are rests entirely on what you chose to believe.

SUMMARY

We develop our concept of God by collecting information and experiences, starting at a young age. Our immediate family, religion, and culture form our first impressions. The rest is up to us. Do we follow the religion of our childhood? Did we have good experiences? Do we explore other ideas, will our family and friends support our search? This is our path forward.

DISCUSSION QUESTIONS

- What are your earliest recollections about God?
- Where did you learn about spiritual or religious topics?
- Have you experienced any extraordinary spiritual experiences?
- How important was, or is, what your family believes a factor in what you believe?
- What do you believe are reliable sources to learn about God?
- What or who do you rely on to protect you from harm?

NOTES

NOTES

LESSON 2

RELIGION AND SPIRITUALITY ARE TWO DISTINCT CONCEPTS

One is eternal and one is not

I wanted to learn more about the difference between religion and spirituality. I knew they were related, but the meanings were blurred. There are multiple definitions for both. In one instance, the focus of spirituality is defined as the connection to God, and religion was the way to provide that connection. Technically, the word religion means a belief, interest, or activities related to God or gods, with many people including spiritual traditions like Buddhism as well. A natural tendency is to link the two, associating one specific religion with an ultimate, universal God. Another description of the two terms is that religion relates to outward, observable behaviors and actions, and spirituality is internal and subjective. Along with that idea, Sandra Schneiders, professor emerita at the Jesuit School of Theology at the Graduate Theological Union, defines spirituality as the integration of one's self "toward the ultimate value one perceives."[1] Although spirituality and religion are straightforward concepts, blurring the differences between them can have profound implications.

Outward religious behaviors are activities such as church attendance, rituals, frequency of prayer, meditation, or any other action an individual associates with their beliefs. These behaviors are easy to observe and measure; for example, the frequency with which someone goes to church, synagogue, or mosque, or how many times someone prays, meditates, chants, and for how long. These are all outward behaviors. However, as we all know, they can be independent of what the person truly believes, thinks, or feels. We have all met or heard about religious people who participate in religious activities or are even revered as godly religious leaders but are later found to be unkind, abusive, or even criminal. These people might appear to be religious but would not score high on anyone's idea of being spiritual.

Levels of spirituality are harder to assess because they are associated with subjective internal states. There are a few validated surveys that attempt to measure characteristics of spirituality such as the purpose and meaning of life, spiritual awareness, and integration of personality. Also, reliable measures have been developed to access an individual's level of spiritual integration. For example, frequency and content of prayer, in addition to an assessment of meaning in life, have been developed to detect changes in people as a result of acute spiritual experiences or spiritual development.[2] Understanding the different meanings between these terms is critical in becoming aware of our spiritual journey.

The distinction between a person being religious and being spiritual becomes evident when we learn about religious people committing atrocities. The Crusades, the Hundred Years' War, child abuse cases, sex scandals, mass murder, and suicides have been committed by religious and assumed spiritual people. This shows that it is possible to be a religious person and yet have no spiritual or godly connection. This is not to say that religion has no meaning. Quite the opposite; many times, our spirituality can only be expressed through religious behavior.

An essential factor in the integration of the two concepts is that religious behaviors are emotionally linked to one's religious belief system. My beliefs brought me to God and God to me. I experienced times of peace and contentment going to Jesus in times of trouble. Also, the wonderful times participating in communion services brought me great comfort by helping me to remember I was on good terms with God. Other non-Christian ideas about God challenged those feelings and attacked my insecurities. That's why I thought the non-Christian beliefs had to be wrong.

From my perspective, it was *The Truth* for me. All other belief systems paled in comparison. It didn't take me long to realize my feelings of certainty stemmed from an emotional connection to my beliefs. Also, what increased my emotional stake was the peace and contentment I sometimes felt when praying, and the calming and reassuring communion services.

These interactions of deeply personal emotions, tied to an organized belief system, are often the foundation of intense religious fervor. They fuel the disagreements, conflicts, and wars existing since the beginning of humankind. I could finally see exactly how this could be, because I vividly remember thinking any other approach to God could not offer what I felt in my heart and knew in my mind. This was my foundation and my rock. Everything else was wrong, wrong, wrong.

At least until I met someone that got me thinking.

SUMMARY

People can be spiritual without being religious, and religious without being spiritual.

DISCUSSION QUESTIONS

- To what degree do you see these concepts as separate? Is it black-and-white, or are the lines blurred?

- Have you known anyone who was religious but not spiritual?

- Have you known anyone that was spiritual but not religious?

- How would you categorize yourself: spiritual or religious, or some combination?

- What do you need to grow in the direction that you want to go? What resources are available to help?

NOTES

NOTES

LESSON 3

THERE ARE MANY WAYS TO GOD

You know the right path for you

During the time I was working through these ideas, I met a woman around my age while I was at a small graphic communications company. She was a freelance writer we hired to assist on a few projects. One day during a break, she mentioned she was a Buddhist. Typically, I would subtly lead the conversation to discuss the differences in our belief systems and explain why my Christian beliefs were better. For some reason, this time, I did more listening than talking. That might have been because she conveyed her thoughts with such sincerity and conviction, it encouraged me to listen. She told me how she was raised as a Buddhist but was also taught about other religions, including Christianity. She described the altar she had in her home, where she went to read and meditate.

She told me how she relied on her Buddhist scriptures throughout her life because they conveyed stories of how other believers overcame suffering and pain.

As I listened, I was fascinated by how similarly we had experienced our religions. At one point, she had tears in her eyes as she told me of how she had relied on her Buddhist practices to get her through a hard time. I could not deny she had experienced much strength when turning to her faith in difficult times, and to her, it was real. I was thinking about that as she presented an idea that made my head spin.

"I know I can get through anything in this life because I have the Buddha in my heart," she proudly stated.

What? I thought to myself. *That's not right.*

"Is something wrong?" she asked, probably reacting to the perplexed look on my face.

"No. Everything's fine," I replied. "I was just thinking about what you just said about having the Buddha in your heart."

"Yes, I know. It's wonderful." Her eyes misted up again. "I don't know how anybody gets by without help from God."

Even though it was brief, the conversation had a huge impact on me. I was stunned that someone could feel as strongly about their religion as I did mine. Part of me was screaming that it was wrong, but another could not deny that her beliefs were real to her. Until then, I had never met anyone that had the same deep personal connection to their religion. I had to know more.

I spent the next several months reading all I could about theories of Buddhism from as many sources as I could find. Some of my preconceived ideas were confirmed, but I also learned many I hadn't known before. The most significant difference was that I was approaching this study with a much more open mind. I felt let down by the narrow perceptions of God I had held and was now able to approach this formerly blasphemous material in a different light. It was refreshing and exciting. I never saw the Buddhist woman again. She had only been hired for that one day; I didn't even get her name.

The two most impactful impressions I gleaned from reading about Buddhism was the dedication to love and compassion, which appeared to be the center of the religion. That was the main goal. "Extinguish hurtful behavior and cultivate loving behavior" was a phrase used many times throughout the literature. The other impression was how many similarities there were between Buddhism and Christianity. An excellent book on this is Thich Nhat Hahn's *Living Buddha, Living Christ.* One comparison can be seen in the teachings of Jesus in the Beatitudes and the Five Precepts of Buddhism, both presenting a description of loving behavior.

THE BEATITUDES — MATTHEW 5:3-11

Blessed are the poor in spirit, for theirs is the kingdom of heaven.

Blessed are those who mourn, for they will be comforted.

Blessed are the meek, for they will inherit the earth.

Blessed are those who hunger and thirst for righteousness, for they will be filled.

Blessed are the merciful, for they will be shown mercy.

Blessed are the pure in heart, for they will see God.

Blessed are the peacemakers, for they will be called sons of God.

Blessed are those who are persecuted because of righteousness, for theirs is the kingdom of heaven.

Blessed are you when people insult you, persecute you and falsely say all kinds of evil against you because of me.

THE FIVE PRECEPTS OF BUDDHISM [1]
Cultivating Compassion
Aware of the suffering caused by the destruction of life, I will cultivate compassion and learn ways to protect the lives of people, animals, plants, and minerals.

Cultivating Loving Kindness
Aware of the suffering caused by exploitation, social injustice, stealing, and oppression, I will cultivate loving-kindness and learn ways to work for the well-being of people, animals, and minerals.

The Oneness of Body and Mind
Aware of the suffering caused by sexual misconduct, I will cultivate responsibility and learn ways to protect the safety and integrity of individuals, couples, families, and society.

Unmindful Speech Can Kill
Aware of the suffering caused by unmindful speech and the inability to listen to others, I will cultivate loving speech and deep listening in order to bring joy and happiness to others and relieve others of their suffering.

Mindful Consuming
Aware of the suffering caused by unmindful consumption, I will cultivate good health, both physical and mental, for myself, my family, and my society by practicing mindful eating, drinking, and consuming.

That was a big concept for me to get over. A non-vengeful God? No Hell? No need for a savior? No need to do anything to avoid eternal punishment?

Another nagging thought I had was about sin in general. What if sin, as I knew it, was not part of the equation? That idea threw me. That and the whole reincarnation thing. While not all Buddhists believe in reincarnation, those that do believe we are all Buddhas and that it takes many lifetimes for us to embrace our true nature and achieve "Buddhahood." We always had this nailed with the Hebrews 9:27 verse, "It is destined for a man once to die and then comes judgment." This proved that reincarnation was not real, at least from the Christian perspective. Some astute non-Christian scholars would challenge me, saying that I couldn't prove or disprove any concept from one or two verses in the Bible. Or that the verse does not specify there is only one life; instead, you are judged after each lifetime. In that scenario, judgment was a review, as compared with eternal salvation or damnation. Throughout the years, I read more about this topic in *20 Cases Suggestive of Reincarnation*,[2] *Many Lives, Many Masters*,[3] and *Journey of the Souls*,[4] among others, that present their research in a reasonable and balanced way. These books contain many examples of how people have been able to recollect living in another time, place, and body. Several examples provide supporting testimonies and compelling evidence. My opinion, after studying several cases, is that it is reasonable to conclude reincarnation may not be true for everyone, but unless the participants jointly fabricated the reports I reviewed, it is hard to deny it occurred with the people in these accounts.

As a result of reading, studying, and talking to scores of people about Buddhism, Eastern philosophy, and reincarnation, I was convinced that other belief systems could be real too, and they could contain at least some aspects of truth. Some of these same truths could also be seen in Christianity, specifically in the teachings of Jesus. This was a breakthrough, and I knew it was a significant departure from my evangelical roots.

Overall, I was energized to learn more about these new concepts, comparing and contrasting them with ideas I had held close for so many years. At the same time, I could not reconcile some of the ideas that most conflicted with Christianity, such as reincarnation and Christianity's perspective on sin. Nevertheless, I felt I was on to something. The most significant theoretical obstacle was the exclusivist references that Christianity was the only way to God, and outside of that there was eternal punishment.

Unfortunately, the enthusiasm of my newfound theological frontier was not shared by everyone. When I attempted to explain what I had been learning, questions would come at me like bullets from a machine gun, especially from my mother. "Where did you get this information?" "How do you know it's true if it's not from the Bible?" I sensed her deep concern and could tell listening to my ideas was disturbing her. I told her I felt as if I was the first person to sail off in the ocean toward the horizon when people believed the Earth was flat.

"Everyone is warning me that I am going to fall off the edge of the Earth to a miserable death," I said. "I'm here to say that I've been past the horizon and back, and it's okay. I'm okay, Mom! I'm not going to burn in Hell; I'm just not!"

My encounter with the Buddhist colleague and subsequent investigations into Buddhism opened my mind to the idea that God was possibly involved in both of these religions. I recounted many of the other religious beliefs I knew about beyond the Judeo-Christian tradition in which I was raised. For example, Catholicism, Mormonism, Presbyterian, Methodist, Lutheran, Pentecostal, as well as non-Christian religions; Islam, the spiritual practices of the American Indians, Hindus, and other Asian religions. As uncomfortable as it was at first, I could not deny there must be something inherently spiritual contained in these beliefs. Most importantly, I would bet that in each of these religious traditions there were genuinely spiritual people as well as hurtful people.

Seeing godly value in other religions, considering moral guidelines outside of the Bible, and investigating other religious perspectives, was clearly beyond the Bible and especially conservative Christian thinking. I was in uncharted waters. The main difference was that now I did not fear I was going to burn in Hell or be rejected by God.

Research related to this can be found in the psychology of religion. Areas of interest in this discipline explore how people gravitate to specific religions out of the approximately 4,200 organized religious groups around the world.

Fascinating research was conducted on this subject by psychologist Steven Reiss and published in 2015 in a book titled *The 16 Strivings for God*, in which he describes how people select the religion that aligns with their specific desires.[5] In his research, he surveyed 7,700 people from diverse backgrounds to better understand common motivational factors and desires. His research showed that people have sixteen basic desires based on their individual psychological needs. He then conducted further analysis to identify correlations to religion. While he admittedly was biased to the Judeo-Christian image of God, his work points out that humans have psychological needs, and many choose specific religions that align with those needs.

16 BASIC DESIRES

Acceptance — the desire for positive self-regard

Curiosity — the desire for understanding

Eating — the desire for food

Family — the desire to raise children and spend time with siblings

Honor — the desire for upright character

Idealism — the desire for social justice

Independence — the desire for self-reliance

Order — the desire for structure

Physical activity — the desire for exercise

Power — the desire for influence or leadership

Romance — the desire for beauty and sex

Saving — the desire to collect

Social contact — the desire to have fun with peers

Status — the desire for respect based on social standing

Tranquility — the desire for safety

Vengeance — the desire to confront provocations

Two thoughts came to mind as I read through Reiss's work. The first was there were probably people that thought the idea of someone picking their religion to fulfill basic psychological needs was blasphemous. According to Reiss's framework, my perception of God fulfilled my needs for *acceptance, curiosity, order*, and *tranquility*. The second thought was even more severe: some people might conclude that this research would support the idea that God was made in the image of man.

At this point in my journey, I knew I was rejecting core beliefs years in development. I noticed, too, that my nagging thoughts grew in frequency and the level of discomfort as well. I wondered why this was happening and found answers in a relatively simple concept.

SUMMARY

Thousands of organized religions exist across the globe, each attracts its followers for different reasons. Many of them claim to have access to ultimate Truth. It is important to understand what your spiritual and emotional needs are so you can choose the best spiritual practice or organization for you.

DISCUSSION QUESTIONS

- Do you agree with the idea that there are many ways to God?

- Whatever your answer, why do you think you believe this? How did you come to this perspective?

- Have you known other people from different faiths than yours?

- Have you had any in-depth conversations with someone from a different faith about their beliefs? What did you learn?

- In your opinion, how best can a person learn about spiritual topics?

- Of the 16 Basic Desires, what are the top three that resonate most with you?

NOTES

LESSON 4
RESOLVING CONFLICTING BELIEFS

It's okay to allow yourself to change

I felt tension caused by differences between my religious beliefs and my internal beliefs, and I wondered how I was going to reconcile them. Living with internal tension is a common experience for many of us. For example, people who work at jobs they dislike or stay in unhappy relationships experience the tension of wanting one thing while struggling to make a needed change. In these situations, people hold their inconsistent feelings in check, sometimes for their entire lives.

The term that describes the tension between beliefs is "cognitive dissonance." This is a situation when a person experiences tension, or dissonance, when considering conflicting ideas or cognitions. One well-known example is the buyer's remorse scenario. Suppose someone is looking to buy a car. They conduct some research, go to the dealer, and sign the papers for their new wheels. When they tell their friend they purchased a car, and the friend suggests another car is safer or more economical, internal tension rises as the buyer considers this new information right after they have committed to buying the new vehicle.

An interesting aspect is if a person perceives a high amount of pressure to maintain their beliefs but then are presented with a competing idea, they experience lower levels of dissonance. Conversely, if a person perceives low pressure to change, they will experience a higher level of dissonance as they struggle to decide what to do. In another car example, suppose a couple is going used-car shopping with a maximum budget of $25,000. When the salesperson shows them a top-line sedan that costs $75,000, they easily turn it down because it dramatically exceeds their budget: low dissonance. When they are shown a new, lower-priced car for $27,000, they experience dissonance because they didn't think they would be able to buy a new car, and it only slightly exceeds their maximum budget.

The level of tension a person can tolerate depends on the individual. Some people can live with it for years, going to a job they hate, remaining in an abusive relationship, or participating in religious rituals they find meaningless. Others, the moment they are unhappy, immediately address the issue.

When thinking about religion, many people are frightened of other belief systems because they cannot cope with the uncomfortable feelings of doubt. Certainly, thoughts of eternal damnation and torture will minimize dissonant feelings of competing religious beliefs held by conservative Christians.

Dissonant feelings are generally reduced in three ways.[1] The first is to simply change the attitude about what is being resisted. In the example of the car purchase, the purchaser could go back to the dealer and get out of the deal and purchase a different car.

The second way people reduce conflicting feelings is to seek out information that supports one of the two conflicting ideas. In this way, a person obtains sufficient evidence to alleviate the tension of conflicting concepts. An example of this is a new mom who believes breastfeeding is healthy and is told by her parents that breastfeeding is not good. Feeling uncomfortable that her parents are opposed to breastfeeding, the new mother experiences dissonant feelings. After researching several articles on the subject, she finds that reputable physicians clearly endorse nursing. The new mother's dissonance is reduced because her position is supported.

The third and most common way people alleviate the uncomfortable feelings produced by dissonance is to trivialize the conflicting attitudes or behaviors. A typical example of this would be a high school student being asked to go to the movies with his friends the night before an important test. Feeling the tension between the two choices, the student reasons that it may not be an important test, or that his average in the class was high and that a low grade on this test would not endanger his overall grade. Deciding the test is not that important, he trivializes the conflicting attitude and enjoys the evening with his friends.

My dissonant feeling increased when I began doubting my beliefs and even more so when I had discussions with my mom. Ultimately, I resolved the dissonance by backing away from fear-based theology, changing my attitude, and giving myself permission to investigate other belief systems.

If you are not one hundred percent comfortable with your religion or spiritual journey, it is essential to understand the source of your dissonant feelings. By working through your doubts to better understand what you believe and why, you will be able to see our own bias and free yourself to change.

This was an important time for me because it helped me reconcile my many nagging thoughts about my beliefs, as well as learn how to handle these uncomfortable feelings. This allowed me to separate myself from my long-held beliefs. After that, I felt free to investigate other perspectives of God and spirituality without fear. I knew now that God was bigger than any religion or theology, with no group having a complete grasp of God.

However, in considering this, I began to wonder, how do we know anything about God? Certainly, most of the world's religions were based on ancient books. We also learn through spiritual leaders and teachers. Some have seen visions or claim to have heard directly from God. The question for me was: how can anyone know for sure? In fact, how do we know anything?

SUMMARY

Awareness of any dissonant feelings with your religion or spiritual life is important for your growth. Understanding how you plan to address these uncomfortable feelings will be your path.

DISCUSSION QUESTIONS

- In your religious or spiritual life, have you experienced doubts or conflicting feelings?

- Have you discussed these with anyone? What were their responses?

- If you do have uncomfortable or dissonant feelings, how have you dealt with them so far (addressed the issue and made a change, gained an understanding of both sides of the issue, or decided the issue was not a big deal)?

NOTES

NOTES

LESSON 5

WHO DECIDES WHAT IS TRUE?

Hint: you do

How do we know anything? I came across this topic in my studies as a general question about the nature of learning. It certainly is a question that directly relates to our understanding of God. According to the many human development models, starting as young children, we build our concepts of God from many sources throughout our lives. But how do we *know* anything? Many theories and models of how we acquire knowledge are covered in the field of *epistemology*, meaning the theory of knowledge. One popular model of knowing is comprised of four perspectives and was introduced by Charles Pierce in 1887.[1]

The first way is by *authority*. This is best described as the only way we learn as a child. This happens mainly with our parents, teachers, and religious leaders. We accept what they say simply and only because they are authority figures. There is no verification, no validation. As children, whatever an authority figure says, we believe it's true.

The second way we know things is through *tenacity*. This is the assurance we give ourselves that once we know something to be true, if new information is presented to the contrary, what we believe remains. Prejudice falls into this category. My struggle with conservative Christian beliefs, family, and friends is an indication of a strong, tenacious level of knowing. Certainly, tenacity was an important component of my beliefs, fueled by the idea that bad things would happen if you doubted or questioned the Plan of Salvation.

The third way we know things is through *a priori* beliefs. This knowing occurs without any direct evidence. Intuition is an excellent example of this type of knowledge. Sometimes you just know something. When someone asks, "How can you be so sure?" The answer usually is, "I don't know why, I just am." Responses like this could be the result of a person having in-depth knowledge of a particular subject, sensitivity to theirs or others' emotions related to the subject, or just having a strong need to be right.

The fourth way of knowing is through *scientific investigation*. This specifically refers to empirical science, meaning that knowledge is gained through observation. An example is of boiling water. A teacher tells us that water boils at 212 degrees Fahrenheit. That is authority. Scientific investigation is obtained when you stick a thermometer into a pot of water, turn on the heat, and observe that it starts to boil at 212 degrees.

While generally considered the most reliable form of knowing, scientific investigation has one limitation, which is that any change must be observable, meaning changes in whatever situation being studied must be able to be seen or measured. The observable change for the boiling water experiment is bubbles of air forming in the water, and the measurement is the temperature. The reason why this can be considered a limitation is that great care must be taken to identify what the expected change will be, in addition to how exactly it will be measured. Otherwise, the scientific conclusion will be considered faulty and inaccurate.

The four ways of knowing can also be applied to our understanding of God and spiritual topics. We all initially learn about God from authority figures. Tenacious beliefs about God are often grounded in our upbringing and solidified with positive experiences of religious traditions, holiday celebrations, and even mystical experiences. Also, the level of tenacious knowing can be enhanced, as mentioned earlier, by theological beliefs stating that doubting a particular belief may be the ticket to an eternity of pain and suffering.

As you might guess, scientific knowing about God and spiritual topics can be controversial. Nevertheless, scores of researchers have been investigating spiritual topics in scientific settings for centuries. The topics investigated have ranged from attempts to "prove" of the existence of God to laboratory settings measuring the effects of prayer on plants, microorganisms, and physical objects. The same scientific challenges come into play with these experiments as with any other. What exactly is being studied? How is it being defined and measured? What are the factors affecting any changes? What factors could be confounding the results?

A priori knowledge of God can be experienced in many ways. The quiet assurance from reading scriptures or singing hymns and the "still small voice" in times of need are a few examples. Although I didn't realize it at the time, it was the intuitive assurance of the born-again Christians in their relationship to God that I initially so desperately wanted. How could they have been so sure? I wondered. The mystical experience was the *a priori* validation I needed to say that I was born again and to be considered a Christian. Interestingly, it was my intuitive nagging thoughts about the judgmental and conditional love of God that hurled me out of organized religion.

People claiming they heard or saw God fuels their commitment to stay close to their chosen traditions and sacred books. This raised a multitude of questions for me. The holy men and women inspired by God to write the scriptures that have been studied for years had to be correct. Right? If this is true, then knowledge about God must be solely based on authority. If so, who were these writers? Did they get it right? I knew of some cultural influences in their writings. Were there other influences? What about the inconsistencies and errors within the scriptures? More so, what about all the different religions whose sacred texts describe God in many different and seemingly incompatible ways?

That was when I realized the basis for any religious belief ultimately comes down to *a priori* belief. There is no way for anyone to objectively know about or prove God exists, let alone understand how we should relate to him or her, or verify that my sins were transferred out of my account, or any other specific religious tenets. Some would even say that *a priori* belief is the most significant component in believing anything, even in our physical universe.

Understanding that knowledge can come from several sources and that knowing is a subjective term, I was able to free myself to look for God outside of the limits of sacred documents and organized religion. Then I began to see God in everything and in everyone.

SUMMARY

There are several ways to identify how we obtain knowledge; understanding how you have decided on your truths can help you evaluate your beliefs.

DISCUSSION QUESTIONS

- Are you aware that you use different ways to determine what you choose to be true (authority, tenacity, *a priori*, investigation)?

- What methods have you used to choose your religious/spiritual beliefs?

- Does one of the perspectives have more importance for you over others?

NOTES

PRAYER: A LIFELINE?

For me, prayer was always a central part of my faith, but also a journey into the unknown. As a child, my efforts began with asking God for things like toys and no cavities at the dentist. As I grew older, my prayers changed from wanting things to wanting direction and clarity in decision-making. While I felt closer to God during those times, I couldn't consistently figure out how to pray and see the results I wanted. It was supposed to be a lifeline to God. My requests related to picking what college to attend or my first job were not clearly answered. The best I could say was that after much consideration and prayer, the decisions were "obvious" to me at the time, which was what I prayed for, but I guess I was looking for something more dramatic. Certainly, my doubts about prayer expanded exponentially when prayers offered during the time my life was imploding went unanswered.

As always, my inner compulsion to know how prayer worked, if it did at all, drove me to spend some time studying the topic in grad school. The first step in this investigation was to see how prayer affected those who prayed, not for others, but themselves. This is known as inward prayer.

INWARD PRAYER

It is important to note that much of the research involving inward prayer can be seen in the reviews of religion and health, specifically religious behavior and health. This is because the behavioral aspects of religion (e.g., church attendance, frequency of prayer, or reading of sacred texts) are seen as being a component of religiosity. However, my interests were in a smaller number of studies that centered on the effectiveness of inward prayer as a single factor.

Reviews of thirty-five studies specifically addressing inward prayer and health included a total participant population of 9,435 and addressed a variety of health-related issues such as pain management,[1] pulmonary disease,[2] length of sobriety,[3] pregnancy,[4] and leukemia,[5] among others. Although the number of studies and participants may seem considerable, it is essential to note that these thirty-five studies occurred over almost fifty years and can be considered scarce. The author of one review, Dr. Michael McCullough from Southern Methodist University, suggests that the low number of studies exist because: a) scholars do not believe it works; b) others do not want to "put God to the test"; and c) limited theoretical definitions make empirical studies difficult.

The author of this review also pointed out that the Judeo-Christian Bible teaches that not all prayer works, with some conditions reported to worsen as a result of prayer. For example, there's the Old Testament story of King David and his son, who was critically ill.[6] King David fasted, prayed, and pleaded with God to spare his child, but seven days later, the child died. When David was told his child was dead, he washed, changed his clothes, and ate. His servants questioned his behavior and asked him how he was able to fast, pray, and plead for his child while alive, and now return to a normal life.

He answered, "While the child was still alive, I fasted and wept. I thought, 'Who knows? The Lord may be gracious to me and let the child live.' But now that he is dead, why should I fast? Can I bring him back again? I will go to him, but he will not return to me."

McCullough explains circumstances may deteriorate even in times of prayer "if persons are led through times of repentance, trial, or 'dark nights of the soul'" as a part of a growing or maturing process.[7]

When we study the results of inward prayer research, the data indicate positive responses in measures of subjective well-being, coping, and psychiatric symptoms. It is essential to note in many of the studies, gender, health, life events, and socioeconomic status were not accounted for and may have impacted the results. As McCullough concluded, "As with most research on prayer and health, uncontrolled confounds compromise the validity of any conclusions."[8]

Interestingly, in a review of prayer research conducted in 2016, twenty years after McCullough published his findings, researchers could only state that prayer "seems to help patients to cope in times of illness and crisis." They continued that more prayer research is needed to determine the impact on patients but can be recommended part of a holistic approach to health.[9]

This was an interesting review and aligned with my conclusions. However, I had more questions. What about praying for others? In the churches and groups, I attended, there were countless requests for prayer for people who were sick or in need. This was the next stop in my prayer research.

SCOTT GUERIN

DOES PRAYING FOR OTHERS WORK?

Many times, when I prayed for someone or heard others say someone needed prayer, I wondered if these efforts had any effect. During my doctoral work, I spent several months researching this topic and learned about seven important studies. The earliest study into the effectiveness of praying for others, or intercessory prayer, was conducted by the Englishman, Francis Galton (1872), and published in his article "Statistical Inquiries into the Efficacy of Prayer."[1] In this report, the author studied the data of life expectancy of clergy and members of the royal houses. These groups were assumed to pray more than the general population and to be supported more through intercessory prayer than anyone else. However, the study results indicated the opposite, with physicians and lawyers outlasting clergy and missionaries not living any longer than commoners. The problem with his study was that the only difference between the groups was the assumed amount of prayer experienced by the clergy, resulting in conclusions that prayer is ineffective. Nevertheless, it was an attempt and a starting point in the study of this phenomenon.

The next study of intercessory prayer was conducted in 1965, with forty-eight patients suffering from progressively deteriorating psychological or rheumatic diseases in a London hospital.[2] The patients were not told they were in any type of study. Prayer groups were assigned to pray for the patients daily for six months. The results showed no significant difference between the two groups. The authors stated that the low number of participants might not have been sufficient enough to detect any differences.

Another study followed four years later in the United States with leukemic children.[3] In this study, ten children with severe leukemia were prayed for daily by families of a Protestant church, while eight similar children were not prayed for, and neither group was told they were in a study. After fifteen months, the mortality rates of the experimental group was 30%, and the mortality rate of the control group was 75%. While the results looked positive, other than the small sample, a significant flaw was that the participants were not matched for the severity of condition. As a result, biological factors may have had a significant effect on the outcomes.

One hundred and sixteen years after Galton published his work, results from a highly publicized prayer study involving humans were presented by Randolph Byrd from the University of California at San Francisco.[4] This study was conducted with 393 coronary care unit patients to determine if intercessory prayer to the Judeo-Christian God had any effect on hospitalized patients. All participants involved, including the hospital staff, knew a study on the impact of prayer was being conducted, though no one knew who was receiving prayers. The intercessors were asked to pray daily for a rapid recovery and prevention of complications and death in the patient.[5]

The results showed the group receiving prayers had a better outcome. The authors summarized that even though prayer by others outside of the study, personal prayer, and strength of religious convictions were not accounted for, "Based on these data, there seemed to be an effect, and that effect was presumed to be beneficial."[6]

Ten years later, a follow-up study was conducted with 999 cardiac patients in a critical care unit of a Kansas City, Missouri hospital.[7] The purpose was to determine whether intercessory prayer reduced adverse effects and length of stay for these patients. The results showed an overall decrease in adverse outcomes with no difference in length of stays.

Another study conducted regarding the effects of intercessory prayer examined the healing effects using a population of forty patients with advanced acquired immunodeficiency syndrome (AIDS).[8] The people providing treatment, called "healers" in this study, were from mixed theistic and non-theistic traditions, including Christian and Jewish intercessors, Buddhist, Native American, Shamanic, graduates from schools of bioenergy, and meditative healing. The healers were given participants on a random and rotating basis for a ten-week period. Each participant was treated by a total of ten different healers for one hour a day, six days per week. The results showed that the twenty patients experienced positive results on six of the eleven outcome measures: significantly fewer outpatient doctor visits, hospitalizations, days of hospitalization, new occurrences of disease, reported lower illness severity levels, and increased levels of mood.

The authors concluded that their studies showed the positive influence of distant healing and urged additional research to be conducted to understand how it works in general, as well as in other health-related applications.

Finally, the findings of the most extensive intercessory prayer study ever conducted were published in late 2006. This was a multimillion dollar study funded by the Templeton Foundation titled "Study of the Therapeutic Effects of Intercessory Prayer (STEP) in Cardiac Bypass Patients — A Multi-Center Randomized Trial of Uncertainty and Certainty of Receiving Intercessory Prayer."[9] The lead researcher was the renowned Herbert Benson, MD, of the Mind/Body Medical Institute, affiliated with Harvard Medical School in Boston. The goal of the study was to observe if intercessory prayer, or the knowledge of it, would affect recovery after bypass surgery. The participants totaled 1,802, with three groups of: 1) 604 receiving prayers after being told that they may or may not be prayed for; 2) 597 not receiving prayers after being told that they may or may not receive prayers and; 3) 601 receiving prayer after being told they would receive prayers.

The agents agreed to pray for fourteen days using the standard phrase for the participant to have "a successful surgery with a quick, healthy recovery and no complications."

Results showed both groups that were told they may or may not receive prayers, with approximately half receiving prayers, had almost the same percentage of complications (51 and 52%). Interestingly, the group that was told they were going to receive prayers and received them had the highest number of complications (59%).

Overall, these studies indicate supplementary intercessory prayer can show no results, or significant improvement, or increased negative results.

One area I was interested in studying was what impact of praying for others has on the people conducting the prayers. This is called the agent effect, and it was a part of my dissertation.

My study was designed to measure the impact of praying or meditating for others on a person's quality of life (QOL).[10] To measure QOL, a validated survey was used that provided ten subscale scores. The agents filled out the survey at the beginning of the study to obtain a baseline QOL score and were provided a target person's first name, last name initial, city, and state. The agents were asked to pray or meditate daily for their target person's general health and well-being. Specific thoughts and amount of time spent was up to them. After four weeks, the agents were given the same survey again to observe any changes in their scores.

At the conclusion of the study, significant improvements were seen in eight out of ten subscale scores in the QOL survey in the agents. The areas of improvement were seen in vitality and decreased bodily pain scores. Other trends of improvement were seen in general health and restrictions as a result of emotional problems.

Spending time reviewing prayer studies was important to me because I was wondering how we can navigate our lives. I considered prayer almost a separate topic from theology and religion and was aware that it had been studied for many years.

My conclusion, after reviewing hundreds of prayer studies for my dissertation, was that, in general, they showed barely significant positive results. A little disappointing, but notable.

One last area to investigate related to prayer I learned about started with my conversation with the Buddhist colleague. Initially, it was an afterthought, but I was surprised to find a host of research had been conducted on the impact of meditation.

SCOTT GUERIN

LESSON 6

MEDITATION IS AN EFFECTIVE WAY TO EXPERIENCE PEACE AND THE PRESENCE OF GOD

It is a common ground between all religions, theologies, and belief systems

Many books, videos, recordings, and cell phone apps are available to provide instruction on a variety of meditation practices. It's easy to be confused and unsure about where to start. One reason for this is that our Western culture does not have much to offer regarding meditation. We are aware of only a few states of consciousness: sleeping, waking, daydreaming, and Spring Break. Religious and spiritual groups in Eastern culture have been exploring states of consciousness for thousands of years.

Initially, in my journey I kept a distance from the topic of meditation. The conservative Christians, in general, shy away from this because meditation is not mentioned to any substantial degree in the Bible and because it has strong ties to Eastern religious practices. This resistance was demonstrated in hundreds of conversations with my mom after I moved away from Evangelical Christianity and organized religion.

"Do you go to church regularly?" Mom asked.

"No."

"Why not?" she replied, squinting at me.

"Because God is right here with us now. He is not contained in a building."

"Do you pray?" she asked, continuing the interrogation.

"Yes, I pray. I've also been trying different types of meditation."

"What do you mean, meditation?" Her brow furrowed, expressing even more skepticism.

"Quieting my mind, listening to soft music."

"So you're a Buddhist now? That's not good," she shot back in an accusatory tone.

"No, Mom, I'm not a Buddhist," I answered, trying to calm her.

"Do you read the Bible?" She continued the line of questioning.

"Yes."

"Good, okay. I'll stop with the questions for now," she concluded with a smile.

The most common method in meditation is concentrating on breathing. Our minds cannot focus on two things at once, so if we focus on our breath, we cannot focus on any other thought. Even people who proudly state they are excellent multitaskers are shifting between two or more subjects very quickly, not simultaneously. Typical meditation exercises suggest taking a long breath in for a count of four and breathing out for the same count. Other methods direct people to breathe in and out for a count of one, then continue with two, up to a ten count, and back down to one. If you break your concentration at any point, you start over again at one until you can complete the full sequence without breaking your concentration.

As I explored different types of meditation exercises, I quickly saw the benefits. I could feel how it calmed me, especially if I was angry or experiencing stress. After maintaining a regular practice of meditation, I was able to concentrate better at work and on other projects and tasks. Fascinated by these results and driven by my innate curiosity, I had to learn more. I used my time in graduate school to review the research around this ancient practice.

The goal of most meditation is the control of brain activity leading to quietness and calming, which positively impacts nervous and physiologic systems. Common elements contained in all varieties of meditation are to increase awareness and bring the mind under conscious control. Individual practices vary regarding the specific imagery, breathing techniques, attentional strategies, and specific goal attributes used, such as increased generosity, love, compassion, or wisdom. Meditative practices to this depth are not usually found in our Western culture. However, some forms of meditation are growing in popularity in our culture and being used in stress management, relaxation, and self-confidence. More intense forms of meditation, called concentration or insight meditation, focus on examining the nature of the mind, consciousness, and expanded awareness.

Many studies with meditation have shown positive results in the treatment of anxiety, social phobia, bronchial asthma, insomnia, reduction of high blood pressure, drug and alcohol abuse, and myocardial infarction, among others. Changes of neural and physiological activities are thought to be accomplished through the use of imagery, calming, and quieting techniques.

Researchers at Harvard Medical School have also studied the impact of meditation. Led by Dr. Herbert Benson, this group identified a meditative state as the Relaxation Response (RR). This is when a person repeats a word, sound, prayer, thought, phrase, or muscular activity, resulting in breaking the normal train of thought. Their studies showed significant reductions in hypertension, cardiac arrhythmias, chronic pain, anxiety, and depression.[1]

In my research on meditation, I learned about a specific practice called Vipassana Meditation, which means to "see things as they really are." Many believe this approach was developed in India by Siddhartha Gautama more than 2,500 years ago. Siddhartha developed a ten-day sequence of activities to promote self-transformation through self-observation. It focuses on the deep interconnection between the mind and body. The method was presented as a "universal remedy for universal ills." Siddhartha used this technique to become "enlightened" and thus became Gautama Buddha, the first Buddha.

Vipassana centers can be found around the world, teaching the same ten-day program used by Gautama. I found one in Shelburne Falls, Massachusetts, and put it on the top of my list of things to do. I soon realized that while the courses are ten days in length, participants are required to arrive one day in advance. This, plus travel back home, meant I needed a total of twelve days to attend the program. It took me eight years before my schedule was clear for the block of time required and I was able to accrue the vacation time. I booked a session one summer in late August.

The first three days of the session were one of the hardest experiences I ever endured. We spent about nine hours a day in a large room, or Dharma Hall, sitting on meditation mats, eyes closed. At times, we received direction on what to concentrate on from the leaders at the front of the room. We had breaks for meals and personal time to walk around the grounds or rest in our rooms. A required component for all participants is to take a vow of "Noble Silence." This means the participant could not bring any reading or writing materials, cell phones, or computers. Eye contact and speaking with others is also prohibited. The purpose of invoking Noble Silence is to help participants be alone with their thoughts in order to achieve the full benefit of the course. After the initial shock of literally no mental activity, I observed my mind slowing and relaxing significantly after day four. Without the deluge of TV, radio, phone, reading, and writing, the pace of the mind slows, but it was an excruciating process for the first few days. However, at the end of the ten days I felt much more emotionally grounded and had a newfound ability to concentrate more deeply and longer than ever before. The feeling for me was as if I had been treading water for some time and was finally able to touch bottom.

Engaging in meditation consistently has had more profound impact on me than any other spiritual or religious experience, practice, or activity. I know that when I am upset, angry, lost, or in need of solace, I can retreat to one or a combination of meditation practices to be restored to a good place once again.

The fascinating aspect of meditation is in its simplicity. Concentrating on breathing, quieting the mind, and mindfulness is the goal. There are no theological or religious requirements in order to engage in this activity and reap the benefits. Anyone in any religion or belief system can participate in one of the many forms of meditation. It is very much ... a common ground.

SUMMARY

Meditation can help you in two powerful ways. First, it will help quiet your mind so that your thoughts will not be bouncing around, commonly known as "monkey brain." The benefit of this is a decrease in anxiety, an increase in peaceful feelings, and an increase in your ability to concentrate. The second way is something that many experienced meditators convey. Through meditation, you train your mind to control your thoughts. When you can choose what you think about, you can control how you feel.

DISCUSSION QUESTIONS

- Meditation has become popular in recent years. Have you tried any methods, classes, or apps? What was your experience like?

- Did it help you in some way? If so, how?

- Do you think meditation competes with religion?

- Do you want to become more experienced in meditation? If so, what resources do you know of that are available?

NOTES

NOTES

LESSON 7

GOD IS STILL COMMUNICATING

Actually, he never stopped

I was in my mid-forties, finishing my graduate studies and writing up my dissertation on the impact of prayer and meditation, when it happened. At that time, I was comfortable distancing myself from conservative Christianity and investigating other religions. I had many discussions with my Buddhist friends, as well as my Muslim and Hindu friends, learning much about the world's largest religions. It was then that I stumbled on something that upended all my thinking.

I was heading back from a weekend in Rhode Island and decided to take a detour north on a winding highway along the Connecticut River. I found a quaint old town right on the river, complete with old churches, a town square, and a two-block shopping area.

Needing a break, I parked and began a slow walk down the well-worn sidewalks. Along the way, I noticed a bookstore and ventured in. This was obviously an old home at one point, with low ceilings, several small adjoining rooms, and squeaky wooden floors. Looking through the bookshelves, I found the psychology section, self-help, then the religion section, my typical stops.

I was about to leave when a book caught my eye that seemed familiar, titled *Conversations with God: An Uncommon Dialogue* by Neale Donald Walsch.[1] I remembered it was on the *New York Times* bestseller list not too long before. My only recollection of it had been that it was some sort of a pop-psychology book on religion, so I wasn't too interested. But I now had some time to kill, since my significant other was only on shop two of many.

As I began to read the first pages, I was surprised to learn the book was about a conversation with God. *Yeah, right*, I thought, recalling the mass suicide of the 913 followers of Jim Jones in Guyana in 1978, the Heaven's Gate cult deaths during Hale-Bopp comet in 1997, and how dangerous it could be to believe people who heard the voice of God. Nevertheless, I read on. Surprisingly, Walsch's story kept my attention as he described his experience.

Over several years, Walsch kept a notepad handy in order to record his thoughts and ideas. It sounded as if it was a form of venting and emotional release for him. It appeared he needed it too. He was frustrated with life, relationships, and work. One night he was in a typical frustrated mood and began to write. Except this time, something else took over the writing. He described it as something took control over his hand, and the words came from somewhere other than him, providing dictation. He was surprised and skeptical at first, but then he surrendered to the process and continued to write. This process resulted in the production of over twenty-one books over several years and a world-wide foundation offering work groups, study groups, conferences, and lectures. The first book focused on individuals, the second on the community, and the third on universal truths and perspectives. The other books discuss both general and specific topics related to life, love, health, wealth, and death, in fascinating detail.

As I read through book one in the store, I appreciated his demeanor and attitude. He stated several times that he did not initially believe this was a conversation with God, that he even questioned his own thoughts and actions during the whole process. I found comfort in not focusing on where the words came from and why he of all people received these "messages," but instead weighed the ideas on their own merit, whatever the source might be. He clearly leaves the decision up to the reader to believe or not believe or to accept or reject the ideas presented in the texts.

This was an important point for me. Just think of all the religions and religious leaders that proclaim they have "The Truth" and that we *must* believe them and join with them or else face the consequences. Certainly, that was what I learned during my Evangelical Christian days, and unfortunately, I was good at conveying that message exceptionally well.

Walsch emphasizes that no one has to, should, or must believe anything he has written. A theme throughout the material is that there is nothing that we should, ought, or must do, or not do. We decide our actions based on the outcomes we want to see.

This material and its origin speak directly to the issue of the validity of the sacred texts of the world's largest religions and how God has communicated with us throughout history. *The Conversations with God* (CwG) material address this topic in-depth throughout the books and includes a detailed discussion in the book, *The New Revelations: A Conversation with God.*[2] Walsch points out the tendency for people throughout history to relegate God's words to ancient texts only. This idea spoke to me because it was something I had often wondered about over the years. Why would God stop communicating? Wouldn't God have something to say to humankind, to his creation, in the last few thousand years? Some sort of reminder, clarification, or application, perhaps? But then I would always revert to what I had been taught and defend the authenticity of the Biblical texts. If these discussions arose, I started with the two New Testament verses:

"Matthew 5:18: I tell you the truth, until heaven and Earth disappear, not the least stroke of a pen, will by any means disappear from the Law until everything is accomplished."

And the second, more ominous verse:

> Revelation 22:18: I warn everyone who hears the words of the prophecy of this book: If anyone adds anything to them, God will add to him plagues described. And if anyone takes words away from this book of prophecy, God will take away from him his share in the tree of life and in the holy city, which are described in this book.

There it was again, the ultimatum used for millennia. Believe this or bear the consequences. At that time, I would go into all the proof texts of the authenticity of the scriptures and how they are reliable Words of God, review the oral tradition, the Dead Sea Scrolls, etc. But what about the sacred books of two of the world's other most popular religions like Hinduism and Islam? Certainly, they had something to offer, even though they contradict each other at the most basic levels. And what about these writings by Walsch? Are these valid? I received an answer in a provocative dialog in *The New Revelations* text where Walsch brings up the matter of scripture validity. I have reproduced it here, beginning with Walsch's question of why anyone would want to read *The New Revelations* book. (The author's questions are in bolded type and the responses follow.)

> **Why would I want to read this book when I've already been told by True Believers that all the answers are in the other books?**
>
> Because you have not heeded them.
>
> **Yes, we have. We believe we have.**
>
> That's why you now need help. You believe you have, but you have not.
>
> You keep saying that your Holy Book (your cultures have many different ones) is what has given you the authority to treat each other the way you are treating each other, to do what you are doing.
>
> You are able to say that only because you have not really listened to the deeper message of these books. You have read them, but you have not really *listened* to them.

But we *have*. We are doing what they *say* we should be doing!

No. You are doing what YOU say that they say you should be doing.

What does that mean?

It means that the basic message of all the sacred scriptures is the same. What is different is how human beings have been interpreting them.

There is nothing "wrong" with having different interpretations. What may not benefit you, however, is separating yourself over these differences, and killing each other as a result of these differences.

That is what you are now doing.

It is what you have been doing for quite some time.

You cannot agree even within a particular group of you, much less between groups, about what a particular book says and what it means, and you use these disagreements as justification for slaughter.

You argue among yourselves about what the Qur'an says, and about what its words mean. You argue among yourselves about what the Bible says, and what its words mean. You argue among yourselves about what the Veda says, what the Bhagavad-Gita says, what the Lun-yu says, what the Pali Canon says, what the Tao-te Ching says, what the Talmud says, what the Hadith says, what the Book of Mormon says...

> And what of the Upanishad, the I Ching, the Adi Granth, the Mahabharata, the Kojiki?
>
> **Okay, we get the point.**
>
> No, actually, you don't. And that's the point. The point is, there are *many* holy writings and sacred scriptures, and you act as if there is only one.
>
> It is *your* sacred scripture that is really sacred. All the rest are poor substitutes at best, and blasphemies at worst.
>
> Not only is there only one Sacred Scripture, there is also one way to *interpret* that Scripture: your way.
>
> This spiritual arrogance is what has caused you your greatest sorrow as a species. You have suffered more—and caused other people to suffer more—*over* your ideas about God than over your ideas about anything else in the human experience.
>
> You have turned the source of the greatest joy into the source of greatest pain.[3]

I was dismayed, thinking that if everyone just went ahead and believed anything they wanted, the world would be in chaos with people fighting over who was right and who was wrong. The people or religion with the most power and money would be the winners. Interestingly, Walsch points out that is exactly what is happening now:

> Your present beliefs are turning your world upside-down. And inside-out. You are tearing yourselves apart, blowing yourselves up, ripping

yourselves to pieces, pulling yourselves in every direction, poisoning yourselves with your beliefs. Your present beliefs are not supporting you; they are killing you.[4]

I read as much of the book as I could that day in the store and bought that copy. Eventually, I bought the entire series and have them on my bookshelf at home. As I read through the CwG books, some of the ideas were strange to me, and at first I didn't know what to make of them, but many of them rang true and resonated with my innermost feelings. Whatever the term was, I had a sense of familiarity with this information that seemed not only to make sense, but in many cases also to verbalize what I had thought for years.

I am not going to review all the CwG concepts and ideas here. I invite you to read any or all of the CwG books or go to their website (listed in the Suggested Readings and Resources in the back of this book) to learn about the CwG material. However, in my journey, these ideas had an enormous impact on me and my beliefs, some of which I will share here.

The crucial point for me was to lay to rest the idea of the punishing and punitive God. I had already come to this conclusion, but these readings helped me to solidify and expand on the concept. It was one of the first nagging thoughts about God I had growing up and all through my conservative Christian years. The idea of God being both loving creator and sustainer of Hell just didn't make sense. Even when I presented the standard line, "I know it sounds harsh, but that's what the Bible says," I didn't totally believe it. Nevertheless, I continued to recite the verses that said all sinners would be punished except the True Believers.

Another idea I had struggled with is that if God is all-powerful, he would not need anything or want anything; therefore, he does not demand anything from us. In the CwG texts, Walsch says that if God demanded anything, it would mean he needed something and therefore was lacking or incomplete in some way. In that light, the whole sin/redemption scenario comes into question. Needless to say, this is a major tenet of all of Christendom and could be unsettling for many. Still, it sounded true to me. For example, if a person had all the money in the world, why would they need more?

I discussed this newfound perspective with a friend of mine who was also a conservative Christian. He responded that God created humankind and our propensity to sin, not because he needed to do it or because he was a mean and insecure deity. It was because he wanted to do it. He agreed God was all-powerful and did not need anything but added that he created us for his pleasure. But to me, needing and wanting can be close in meaning. Something seemed lacking and incomplete in either case. After thinking about this for a while, even if this conventional definition of God did not portray Him as a mean deity, it at the very least portrayed Him as a cruel prankster. In this perspective, God created the Garden of Eden then placed Adam and Eve in it, telling them not to eat of the tree of the knowledge of good and evil. Knowing that Adam would falter, God waited for the apple to be eaten and then, bam, that was it, they were banished out of the garden, and the rest is history. And all this was for God's pleasure? That is a strange type of love, and I could no longer embrace the idea.

This type of "believe in a certain way or else" scenario is pointed out by Walsch as the basis of fear-based religions where God is punishing, punitive, vengeful, and jealous. Many times, I was told God loved us unconditionally and that we should be grateful He did. However, the reality presented in the Christianity I was raised in claimed that His love was quite conditional. If God was God, I thought, how could he be hurt? Why would he be angry? Sometimes I thought that if the God I learned about in the Bible was a real person, he would be a jerk.

Walsch presents an interesting perspective on how religion has misread the nature of God. He offers this in the form of "Five Fallacies about God." When religious groups adhere to these fallacies, it creates crisis, violence, killing, and war.

FIVE FALLACIES ABOUT GOD[5]

First, you believe God needs something.

Second, you believe that God can fail to get what he needs.

Third, you believe that God has separated you from Him because you have not given Him what he needs.

Fourth, you believe that God still needs what He needs so badly that God now requires you, from your separated position, to give it to him.

Fifth, you believe that God will destroy you if you do not meet His requirements.

Reading through the CwG materials, I became convinced God communicates with us in many ways now, today and every day. He is not impotent, as many religions proclaim, and limited to ancient texts and interpretations from only a specific and educated few. Not only that, but I now saw that He communicates with us in other ways, in addition to the Bible. And that is one of the foundational messages of the CwG texts, that God is still communicating with us. In fact, God never stopped.

One other significant idea in the CwG material took me a while to fully accept. This is the idea that there is no such thing as right and wrong. At first, this sounds absurd. I thought some things have to be right and other things must certainly be wrong. If not, then nothing would matter; the world would be in chaos. Walsch understands the impact of this idea and continues to explain the meaning as it is applied in an ultimate sense. For example, if a person lives in New York City, wants to go north to Boston, and begins their journey traveling directly west to Pennsylvania, they are not necessarily wrong; they are simply traveling in a direction that will not get them where they want to go. From a personal perspective, if a person wants to have a good marriage and rich family life, they will not go on every business trip offered or stay out late at night with friends several times a week. Going on trips and staying out late are not bad in and of themselves, but if a person wants to have a solid family life, they may want to reconsider their lifestyle. Just like a person heading to Pennsylvania might want to consider changing direction if they want to go to Boston. Neither is definitively "wrong"; they simply are not acting in a way that supports what they ultimately want to do.

This way of looking at things makes much more sense to me now, but in the Christian fellowship group in college, we were taught that this type of thinking was not good. The term that this would fall under was "moral relativism." This indicated a person was viewing the world on a sliding scale of morality and not adhering to the moral laws of God and Christianity. It was a bad position to hold and meant the person either did not know God or did not believe what the Bible said about sin, weakening the need for redemption. However, even back then, I had some nagging thoughts about this perspective of morality. I wondered if the hardline approach was true. One example I thought about many times was the Fifth Commandment. "Thou shall not kill." This is a straightforward statement, but was it really true? We all believed the Bible in this proclamation. We should not kill anyone, right? No, never, was the typical answer. This was because the word "kill" most likely referred to murder, premeditated murder, perhaps. Killing in self-defense was acceptable, with varying degrees of acceptance of manslaughter depending on the seminary your pastor was from or the congregation's view. Besides, you may need to kill those who are threatening our freedom or faith in times of war. To me, that was moral relativism, spoken by those who supposedly opposed it. It never made sense to me.

As a child, I was taught that we had to "be good," "don't sin," and "do the right thing," with varying degrees of "or else" looming in the background. Even when I considered myself a Christian, there was the concern of punishment because I was still a sinner. The God I knew, while forgiving, was also severely and eternally judgmental.

Considering the idea that there was no right or wrong rang true to me, allowing me to be myself without fear of repercussions. Well, at least outside the consequences of my actions, which was fine. I felt free. The sin factor was no longer in the way. This is how God could love us unconditionally.

SUMMARY

God, Spirit, or the Universe did not stop communicating centuries ago. Messages of love, support, and guidance surround us from many sources. We just need to listen.

QUESTIONS

- Did the conversation Walsch had with God resonate with you?

- What do you agree with? What don't you agree with?

- Do you think God communicates with us now? If so, how?

- Have you experienced a situation where God or the Universe communicated with you in some way? If so, describe what happened.

NOTES

LESSON 8

THERE IS NO SEPARATION BETWEEN GOD AND US

We are a part of God

The *Conversations with God* material presents alternative and insightful ways to view our world individually, as a group, and universally. Another book addressing similar issues was published a few years before the CwG books, *A Course in Miracles* (CM) by Helen Schucman and William Thetford. Both were professors of medical psychology at Columbia University's College of Physicians and Surgeons in New York City.[1] The authors held conservative and atheistic beliefs and worked in a highly academic and prestigious setting. The content of their book was received similarly to Walsch's. Schucman and Thetford described the process as "a kind of rapid, inner dictation" written in shorthand notebooks. They, as with Walsch, were initially skeptical and had a difficult time accepting what was happening as the unusual process continued.

The topics covered in the CM material parallel the CwG books to a striking degree. One difference is that it is presented in the Christian setting with many references to Christ, God, and the Holy Spirit. In this way, it is much more palatable to the Christian tradition. Another difference is that the ideas are presented in a technical step-by-step format, whereas the CwG material is a narrative format. I refer to the CwG books as an "owner's manual" style and the CM as a shop manual. The CM material presents a thought-by-thought analysis of how we think about God and ourselves, including exercises to help assimilate the concepts.

The CM text suggests the main problem today relates to the incorrect perception of separation between God and us. The book proposes a solution is to reject our misperceptions of the world as being apart from God in order to see the Truth. The truth is Love, and according to the authors, Love is all there is. In their view, sin is defined simply as a lack of love. According to the book, our view of the world is clouded by perceptions subject to the effects of time, change, beginnings, and endings, and based on interpretations. These interpretations come only from us, from our internal frame of reference, and are subjective, meaning that we create our world based on our ideas of it. By seeing the world as it really is, we can forgive and accept the world and create unity between us and God. In fact, the authors state that forgiveness is our only function. It is the only way we can be reunited with God and each other. While the book is written in an academic and cerebral tone, many points are helpful. For example, some of the lessons center on ideas many of us can relate to such as, "I am never upset for the reason I think,"[2] or "I am upset because I see what is not there,"[3] or "I see only the past,"[4] or "My thoughts are images that I have made."[5]

The idea that there is no separation between God and us is not new and is embedded in several of the world's religions. Several references to our oneness with God can be found throughout the Bible. For example, in the book of John, chapter 17 verse 11, Jesus is praying before he was arrested and asked God to "…protect them by the power of your name—the name you gave me—so that they may be one as we are one." And continues in verse 22:

> I have given them the glory that you gave me, that they may be as one as we are one: I in them and you in me. May they be brought to complete unity to let the world know that you sent me and have loved them even as you have loved me.

Dr. Wayne Dyer, a popular author on spirituality, expands on this idea by developing a list of phrases indicative of how various religions have conveyed the concept of unity and an intimate connectedness with the "source."

> Christian—The Kingdom of God is within you.
>
> Islam—To know yourself is to know God.
>
> Buddhism—Look within, you are the Buddha.
>
> Hindu—By understanding yourself, all the universe is known.[6]

Obviously, the implications of no separation between God and us are monumental. In Christianity, everything is tied to the idea that we sinned in the Garden of Eden and we have been trying to get back in God's good graces ever since. It also sets up the prime dilemma: if the separation is not addressed, then it's eternal damnation. The idea that the separation doesn't exist changes everything. When discussing this idea with my Christian friends, many asked the question: "Suppose you are wrong?" At first, my cognitive dissonance was high; now, it's low. One of the most powerful reasons for that is that in times of prayer, and more so in meditation, I now feel that I am a part of everything.

What I admire almost as much as the ideas themselves in both the CwG and CM is the way the material is presented. In both books, the content is presented with an attitude of openness, offering the reader an opportunity to make their own decisions about the ideas. No threats, no punishment, just conveying ideas about life in an atmosphere of loving kindness.

The CwG material and the CM were important for me in that they presented a comprehensive approach not only to who God is, but also who we are. This was accomplished outside of all organized religious settings.

SUMMARY

Realizing there is no separation between God and us is startling at first, and we resist the thought. Through the silence of prayer, meditation, and the sounds of nature, we can feel the connection.

QUESTIONS

- Where do you think the idea of separation from God came from?
- What would no separation from God mean to you?
- What would you do differently, assuming this is true? How would it impact your life?

NOTES

NOTES

LESSON 9
VALIDATING BELIEF SYSTEMS

A word about automatic writing

When I read Walsch's account of how he developed the CwG material, I was skeptical to say the least. According to Walsch, his hand began writing on the notepad he had used to record his frustrations and questions. How did that work? Did his hand just take off on its own? Could he stop it if he wanted to? The same questions come up with Helen Schucman's recounting of how the CM content was written. There are other cases, too. For example, the Seth material dictated by Jane Roberts to her husband from 1963 to 1984. Roberts claimed the content was given to her from a nonphysical entity named Seth.[1] A more bizarre example is Hélène Smith (real name Catherine-Elise Müller), a French medium in the late nineteenth century who claimed she received messages from Mars in a Martian language.[2]

From my perspective, the way in which Walsch and Schucman reacted to their experiences provides enormous validity. The authors clearly conveyed how surprised they were when they started receiving and recording the material and even doubted their own authenticity. Most importantly, they offer their content as a take-it-or-leave-it manner by encouraging the reader to try it out and see what they think. This is quite the opposite of the threats of punishment or abandonment maintained by many of the fear-based religions and cults, insisting that their way is the Truth to be followed without exception or question. Finally, as I considered their ideas, it simply made sense and resonated with me. Also, and this is not something I share often, but much of the material in the CwG book felt familiar to me, as if I was rereading it.

While not claiming it was dictated or transcribed in an automatic writing fashion, most adhering to the Evangelical Christian tradition accept the Bible as the Word of God without question. The scripture verse or "proof text" most often quoted is in the New Testament second book of Timothy 3:16: "All scripture is inspired by God and is useful for instruction, for conviction, for correction, and for training in righteousness." The important word here is "inspired," and referring to the original Greek language in which the text was written, the word is θεόπνευστος or theopneustos, which literally means "God-breathed," *theos* meaning "God" and *pneu* meaning "to breathe." This text is used as the cornerstone in many fundamentalist and Evangelical Christian churches, schools, and other organizations and often emphasizes the Bible as containing the Truth, the literal Word of God. Many Christian organizations require potential members to sign a Statement of Faith indicating they believe the Bible to be without error, solidifying the idea that the Bible is not from the hand or mind of humans, but rather from a divine source. Signing a Statement of Faith is a strong reinforcement of tenacious knowing, because the person signing is publicly committing themselves to a specific set of beliefs.

It is important to note that the idea of information coming from outside a person occurs in other disciplines as well. One well-known example is Albert Einstein. Born in a Jewish family, his interests in religion expanded to his scientific beliefs. However, in his perspective on the connection of science and divinity, he appeared to blur the lines between humanity and something larger. For example, these two quotes[3]:

> "There remains something subtle, intangible and inexplicable. Veneration for this force beyond anything that we can comprehend is my religion."

> "When the solution is simple, God is answering."

Another remarkable example of content coming to a person from outside themselves is in the life of Srinivasa Ramanujan in the early part of the twentieth century. Ramanujan's story was conveyed in the book *The Man Who Knew Infinity* by Robert Kanigel and the subsequent 2015 movie directed by Matt Brown.[4]

Raised in the impoverished city of Madras, India, Ramanujan was struggling to make a living in menial jobs when an employer noticed he had exceptional skills in mathematics. His employer was so impressed, he sent samples of Ramanujan's mathematical work to the renowned mathematician G.H. Hardy at Cambridge University in hopes Ramanujan would be recognized for his talent. The plan worked. Ramanujan moved to Cambridge, and after several years struggling with a foreign culture and lack of formal academic training, he was accepted as a fellow of the college.

The fascinating part of this story related to the ongoing conflict Hardy and Ramanujan engaged in throughout his years at Cambridge. The disagreements centered on Ramanujan's inability to provide the backup work or proofs that typically support complex mathematical formulas in academic settings. While many of the academics at Cambridge agreed that Ramanujan's work was exceptional and at a near-genius level, the lack of back-up work was causing great consternation. For a long time, Ramanujan refused to tell Hardy how he was able to produce such exceptional work, until one day he explained that he received his inspiration and understanding from a divine source. The answers came to him when he dreamed he was in the presence of the god Narasimha and "scrolls containing the most complicated mathematics would unfold before his eyes."[5] This divine goddess showed Ramanujan the formulas, and he understood them. The struggle was in showing how current mathematical theories were connected to his answers. Ramanujan conveyed an interesting thought that mimics Einstein's quote: "An equation for me has no meaning unless it expresses a thought of God."[6]

There are other examples of humans claiming to receive inspiration and even direct communication from sources seemingly outside of themselves, some occurring within the Christian tradition. One is the phenomenon of speaking in tongues recorded in the New Testament in the book of the Acts of the Apostles. The narrative states that approximately fifty days after Jesus came back to life and ascended into Heaven, the Holy Spirit descended on the disciples in the form of tongues of fire, which appeared over each of them as they began to speak in several different languages. Other accounts in the Bible state the sounds were unintelligible. This practice occurs today in Christian Pentecostal churches, although the exact practice and format is not consistent and can be controversial.

So, what can we make of these external sources of inspiration, communication, and information? Are they from God, alien beings, or some sort of higher level of our collective consciousness? Assuming the authors were not psychotic, delusional, or drugged when they recorded their content, are the sources the same or different? And can we be sure the authors wrote down the thoughts without imposing any of their own biases or beliefs? It's an important point to remember — this same scrutiny can and should be applied to all the religious texts and experiences found in the world's organized religions, as well as those outside the main religions such as the texts of Neale Donald Walsch, Schucman, or Ramanujan.

The nine hundred followers of Jim Jones and his Peoples Temple were apparently convinced that taking the cyanide-laced punch was a good idea at the time but ended up being participants in the Jonestown Massacre of 1978. There are many other examples, spanning religious and nonreligious groups led by charismatic leaders who exploit, harm, and brainwash their followers to give their time, money, and even their lives to whatever cause they are promoting. This leaves the rest of us wondering how anyone could be duped to such an extreme degree to buy into such nonsense. However, just as this has happened in the past, it will happen in the future. But how can we determine the good from the bad? The real from the fake?

Criteria that can be used to evaluate these various sources are simple. The first is a lack of demands any organization imposes on people. Certainly, most fear-based religions contain mandates in order to be accepted by God, to avoid punishment, Hell, or damnation. In light of that, the take-it-or-leave-it approach, for me, provides strong validation. People of any organization or belief system should be able to believe, doubt, come, go, or participate to whatever degree they prefer, without fear of retribution. Another way to assess whether a belief system is founded on positive principles is to compare it with the attributes presented in the New Testament book 1 Corinthians 13:4–7. These verses are presented at many Christian weddings as the fifteen-point definition of love. Gauging how these characteristics are embedded, or not, in a belief system can provide a good way to evaluate its core principles.

The 15-point Definition of Love

1. Patient
2. Kind
3. Does not envy
4. Does not boast
5. Not proud
6. Does not dishonor others
7. Not self-seeking
8. Not easily angered
9. Does not delight in evil
10. Keeps no record of wrongs
11. Rejoices with the truth
12. Always protects
13. Always trusts
14. Always hopes
15. Always perseveres

SUMMARY

Pray for the courage to be true to yourself. Follow your inner calling to God and Spirit. Trust that you know love so well, you will reject everything else.

QUESTIONS

- What do you think about the idea that God or someone else is speaking to us through different people?

- Do you think others are delivering messages to us?

- What do you think about the fifteen ways to validate messages and behaviors of those who claim they are speaking for God?

- Are there other ways to determine this?

- Why do you think people follow those who take advantage of or harm others?

NOTES

LESSON 10

WE ARE ALL ANGELS

We are spiritual beings living a temporary physical existence

Understanding that my strivings for God originated from my psychological drives of *acceptance, curiosity, order, and tranquility*, I could see how my initial religious beliefs addressed these needs, especially the need for *order*, because it reconciled the sin, eternal judgment, and forgiveness equation. However, after several years of trying to force-fit everyone into a rigid belief system, the same strivings that led me to Evangelical Christianity propelled me to seek answers beyond religion.

Embracing the idea that God was still communicating with us was one of two milestone insights for me. The content presented in CwG and CM rang true, and I felt comfortable about their sources, even though they were outside the Bible. I was finally free from organized religion and open to exploring other ideas about God.

The other breakthrough was accepting the idea that we are not separate from God. We are expressions of God, children of God. We are angels and messengers of God. This means that sin is not in the equation, and therefore there is no need for salvation. There is nothing to be saved from.

"How do you know you are not going to Hell?" Mom asked during one of our discussion/interrogation sessions. Her typically squinty eyes peered at me.

"Because I just know. I do not believe God is judgmental, and his love is not conditional."

"What do you mean?" she shot back, as usual.

"Okay, maybe this will help. Let me ask you a question. Is there anyone on this planet who can say I am not your son?"

"Of course not," she replied.

"Is there anything I could do that would cause you or Dad to say I am not your son?"

"No, never. Of course not," she affirmed.

"That is the best example of my relationship with God. That is unconditional love and acceptance. I have no fear of judgment. Everything I go through in this life or after I die is all about learning and growth."

"So you don't have to do anything? Go to church, read the Bible, pray to Jesus?" Her anxiety level was rising, her voice shaky.

"I can do these things, and I do. I enjoy doing them. I just don't *have* to do them to appease God."

Blank stare from Mom.

"Here's another example. Remember that time I was playing and I knocked over that vase Grandma gave you?"

"Yes, your father and I were very upset," she recalled.

"Yes, you were. You sent me to my room and no TV for a week. But suppose every week after that for months I came to you and Dad asking for forgiveness. And I would plead 'I'm clumsy, I break things, and please forgive me.'"

"We would say we forgave you, but after a few weeks, we might wonder if there was something wrong with you. We might send you to a shrink." This she said with a smirk because she knew it would get to me.

"Well, the term is psychologist, but yes, something would be wrong, wouldn't it?"

"Yes, a child should have no doubts their parents love them," she said confidently.

"But at the same time, we go to church every week confessing to God we are sinners deserving punishment, asking for forgiveness. Every week. But that is not what God is like; he is like a parent with a child. I have no doubts that you and Dad love me, and that God loves me too."

"Wow, that is really something, Scott. I don't know what to think about this," she said, looking into the distance. "I just hope you're okay."

"Yes, Mom. I'm okay. I love you."

"I love you too, boy. My youngest son," she said as we hugged goodbye.

These insights, combined with my experiences and what I learned, were all aligned. I realized I was truly a part of God; there was no separation. There is no sin or need for forgiveness. We are all divine beings on a journey to learn how to be more loving and less hurtful, and the journey can span hundreds of lifetimes.

Our place in this, as described by Dr. Dyer, is that "We are all spiritual beings living a temporary physical existence." This statement suggests that we transition between physical and spiritual lives to learn and to help others. Neale Donald Walsch also proposes that we are on an evolutionary path through many lives to learn how to exemplify positive virtues, as do almost all Eastern religions.

This is not a slightly different view of God, but a huge departure from many of the belief systems that have been embedded in human culture for centuries. Paradigm shifts on this scale have happened before. For example, when Galileo proclaimed Copernicus was correct that the Earth revolved around the sun. As we all know, Galileo was convicted of heresy for publishing these radical thoughts and died while under house arrest in 1642. What is more amazing is that it took over seventy years from when Copernicus first published his theories to when Galileo presented his supportive findings. Paradigm changes take time.

Most importantly, challenges to long-standing concepts are typically met with resistance. As stated by the famed Irish playwright, George Bernard Shaw, "All major changes in thought begin as blasphemy."

SUMMARY

The Sanskrit word *namaste* has several English translations and is used as a greeting. The one I like the best is "the God in me sees the God in you." Seeing everyone as spiritual beings, as angels, disrupts all the ideas of separation that humans like to maintain.

QUESTIONS

- What do you think of the idea that you are an angel, a part of God?
- Have you known or seen others that would be better examples?
- What would a person that is an angel look like in your mind?
- Does an angel always have to be perfect?
- Can an angel be on a learning curve?

NOTES

NOTES

LESSON 11

THE LAW OF ATTRACTION

A universal explanation?

The next challenging question I began to wrestle with was: if we are angels and not separate from God, who should we pray to to get what we want to be, do, or have? I knew from reviewing hundreds of studies on prayer that the results were not as consistent as one would hope. Was there an alternative to prayer that might fit this new paradigm? As has happened at other times in my life when struggling with a question, I would stumble onto something that helped me find the answer. This time, I stumbled on the Law of Attraction (LoA).

The LoA, also known as the power of intention, is the idea that we create all experiences in our lives by applying consistent thoughts and feelings about each aspect. For example, if we want to have a job that is positive and interesting, if we consistently picture ourselves in a position we want, eventually the opportunity will present itself. Or, if a person regularly complains about their job, telling others how bad it is, they will remain in that unpleasant situation. In its most simplistic form, the term "what goes around, comes around" captures this idea. I believe there is something worth exploring in the LoA. In this chapter, I will review the concept from the viewpoints of different authors.

I learned about the LoA when the book *The Secret* by Rhonda Byrne became popular after its release in 2006. It was getting some play in the press after being on the *New York Times* bestseller list for 190 weeks. What puzzled me was not the length of time on the list, but at what point in time would this no longer be a secret. I continued to be intrigued by the attention surrounding the enormously popular secret message.

In the first few pages of the book, Byrne explains that her life was in a state of ruin when her daughter gave her a book written in 1910 by a little-known author. The book was *The Science of Getting Rich* by Wallace D. Wattles. After Byrne read about the concepts presented by Wattles, she conducted extensive historical research to see if these concepts were present in any other philosophies, religions, or cultures. The results of her research proved fruitful, and she then developed the content of *The Secret*, eventually translated into over forty languages, along with the development of several companion books.

The concepts Wattles presented are both simple and revolutionary. Similar to the CwG material, they represent a significant step away from the theological frameworks of the world's largest organized religions (Christianity, Islam, Hinduism, and Buddhism), yet according to Byrne, components from the core tenets of these religions are embedded in *The Secret's* ideas. The fundamental concept of Wattle's work revolves around the idea that we can get whatever we want through wealth and that obtaining wealth is accomplished by "...doing things in a Certain Way."[1]

Wattles' idea of a Certain Way is contained in three points repeated several times throughout his book.

> There is a thinking stuff from which all things are made, and which, in its original state, permeates, penetrates, and fills the interspaces of the universe.
>
> A thought, in this substance, produces the thing that is imagined by the thought.
>
> Man can form things in his thought, and, by impressing his thought upon formless substance, can cause the thing he thinks about to be created.[2]

The term Law of Attraction is not contained in Wattles' work, but the concept is presented throughout. One aspect that Wattles emphasizes in his work is often left out of other LoA content; that action is critical for the process.

"By thought, the thing you want is brought to you; by action you receive it."[3]

According to Wattles, thought alone will not magically make something physically appear in front of you, but circumstances will come together serendipitously to bring you what you have been envisioning. He provides an example of a person who wants a new sewing machine. If a person holds a detailed mental image of a sewing machine, coupled with the feeling of unquestionable certainty, it will come to them. Possibly, they will meet someone who happens to have a sewing machine for sale, or some other opportunity will appear where a sewing machine will become available. So, in Wattles' perspective, thoughts bring about the opportunity, but the person still has to act to obtain what they want. In this example, the person has to take the action of connecting with the owner of the sewing machine, getting the money, and arranging to meet and completing the transaction.

Another significant source of information on the LoA comes from a different realm. Wanting to learn more, I quickly found a significant source of information in the LoA material developed by Esther and Jerry Hicks. The authors produced several books, audiotapes, videos, and conducted hundreds of workshops throughout the United States. Since the Hickses published their work in the late eighties, several years before *The Secret*, I focused on their work next.

In their book, *Ask and It Shall Be Given*, the Hickses explain how they developed the content of the LoA. The process was similar to Walsch's experience in writing the CwG books, through an automatic writing process. Esther initially typed the content as the words came to her, and later she would verbalize the material directly. One big difference is that while Walsch presents his source as God, Esther reported her source was a group of nonphysical beings or entities. These entities were never in physical form and communicated collectively as one voice calling themselves Abraham.[4]

The Hickses generated a massive number of materials related to the LoA, addressing many aspects of the concept, far too many to discuss here. However, I will present a few of their concepts, and I encourage any seeker to learn more through their books and website, listed at the end of this book.

In their work, the Hickses expand on Wattles' concept of impressing thoughts upon formless substance, resulting in bringing thoughts to fruition. They explain that this phenomenon impacts our lives and our world, whether we are aware of it or not.

The Hicks' concept of the LoA is defined as, "That which is like unto itself is drawn." The first time I learned of this idea, my thought was this was contradictory to basic magnetism. With hundreds of hours playing with magnets of all shapes and sizes when I was young, I knew that it was the opposite poles of a magnet that attracted each other, and the like poles repelled. On the other hand, I could see how similar things have a tendency to be grouped together, such as how like-minded people are often attracted to each other, and we tend to notice characteristics in others that reflect our attributes. Harmonic resonance is sometimes mentioned in discussions about the LoA as an example of like attracting like. Harmonic resonance is when an object vibrating at a specific frequency is placed near another similar object, and it, the second object, begins to vibrate at the same frequency as the first. Tuning forks are good examples; if you tap one and move it to another that was not tapped, the second tuning fork will begin to vibrate at the same frequency as the first. While this does not prove what the LoA authors are describing, it is a good analogy for the concept.

According to the Hickses, "every thought vibrates, every thought radiates a signal, and every thought attracts a matching signal back."⁵ The authors provide an example of a radio tower transmitting a signal at a specific frequency and a radio being tuned to that exact station. When the transmitter and the receiver are mismatched, nothing happens, but when they are in alignment, the music flows. So it is with our thoughts; whatever we give our attention to emits a vibration that attracts the object of our thoughts.

According to the authors, the quickest way to experience what you want is to hold consistent positive thoughts to attract it into your life, to imagine having it, and pretend it's already yours, and you are enjoying the experience. Practicing these thoughts also helps to provide a consistent vibrational offering of attraction.

This is almost identical to Wattles' idea that holding a detailed image in mind with certainty will provide what the person is envisioning. Hicks also emphasizes the LoA is in effect at all times whether a person is consciously focusing on something or not. This means that if a person is consistently ruminating about their *old broken-down car*, then they will continue to experience their *old broken-down car*, or if a person keeps dreaming about their wedding day having perfect weather, then they will experience ideal weather.

SUMMARY

The LoA provides a possible explanation about how many things work. In a sense, we are in a sea of energy that we manipulate either consciously or unconsciously. Like a sailboat, we navigate this world through our thoughts and intentions. Once we understand this, we can be the *captain of our fate and the master of our souls.*

DISCUSSION QUESTIONS

• Does the Law of Attraction resonate with you in any way?

• Have you thought about, wished for, or prayed for anything specific that came to be? If so, please describe it.

• Do you think there is any connection between prayer and the Law of Attraction?

• Do you think your thoughts can influence situations and coincidences to occur?

• Do you think your thoughts can impact your physical world?

NOTES

NOTES

HOW THE LAW OF ATTRACTION WORKS

In the numerous materials presented by the Hickses, many descriptions, explanations, exercises, and tools are provided that illustrate how the concept of LoA works and how to apply it in real-life situations. I found three points especially interesting related to how the LoA works, and, importantly, why it doesn't work.

One reason why the LoA doesn't work is a lack of clear and consistent thoughts. Many times, people get distracted and stop thinking about a particular thing or lose interest. Another way the LoA would not appear to work is when even if clear and consistent thoughts are maintained, thoughts of uncertainty and doubt cancel out the overall vibration of the specific desire. A third reason, which was most interesting to me, is that many times people are not aware that what they are focusing on, vibrating, and manifesting about is, in fact, the opposite thing they want to experience in their lives. For example, if a person consistently is thinking, "I want more money," or "I want to have a better job," the vibration that will manifest is the "I want" part. So, as long as the person concentrates on *wanting* to have money or a better job, that feeling of *wanting* will continue, and nothing will change. You can see why picturing yourself as *having* the thing or situation you want, and practicing these thoughts is so critical.

The Hickses state that another important component of how the LoA works relates to emotions. The authors present the idea that our emotions are a sixth sense, just as taste, touch, smell, sight, and hearing are senses. The main difference is that the five physical senses relate to our physical experience, and emotions relate to who you are at your deepest levels — your *source*. The first step is to become aware of your emotions and specific feelings, and the second is to gain the ability to change your emotions to align more with what you want to do, be, or have.

To present their concepts, the authors provide examples of how we can improve our point of attraction, meaning how to think best and control our feelings to attract what we want in our lives. In *Ask and It Is Given*, the authors provide twenty-two examples to help a person improve their "point of attraction." The examples outline ways to visualize what we want and show how we can monitor and change our feelings to align with our vision.

They begin by introducing the idea of assessing our emotional "set point," which is to identify how we are feeling at the moment precisely. The authors provide a sample range of twenty-two emotional descriptions from the highest most positive emotions to the lowest.[1]

A SCALE OF EMOTIONS

1. Joy/Knowledge/Empowerment/Freedom/Love/Appreciation
2. Passion
3. Enthusiasm/Eagerness/Happiness
4. Positive Expectations/Belief
5. Optimism
6. Hopefulness
7. Contentment
8. Boredom
9. Pessimism
10. Frustration/Irritation/Impatience
11. "Overwhelment"
12. Disappointment
13. Doubt
14. Worry
15. Blame
16. Discouragement
17. Anger
18. Revenge
19. Hatred/Rage
20. Jealousy
21. Insecurity
22. Fear/Grief/Depression/Despair/Powerlessness

12 LESSONS

By identifying our starting emotional status as a baseline, we can not only choose the example that best matches our emotional level at the time, but we can also assess how effective the exercises are in elevating our emotional status. For example, the exercise titled "Finding the Feeling Place" is designed for people who want to improve their situation to receive more money, a better job, happier relationship, or better-feeling body. This exercise is meant for people who have an emotional baseline or set point on the low end of the scale of between #9 Pessimism to #17 Anger. The goal of this exercise is to create images of the times when you had what you now want or to envision yourself having them. In other words, spend time in the *feeling place* that you want. The authors mention taking small steps, not leaps to increase emotional levels gradually. By doing this, your emotional set point will improve.

Interestingly, the Universe, according to the authors, does not discern whether the vibrations offered are from an actual life situation, or if it is imagined. In either case, it will provide according to the vibrations offered. The idea of projecting oneself into a desired experience is also depicted in the familiar term "fake it until you make it," found in other self-help programs.

The authors' explanation of coupling a precise and consistent vision of what we want with equally consistent feelings is like a sculptor who learns to mold clay into the piece they want to create. According to the authors, this is how we shape our lives out of the people we meet and the events and opportunities we experience.

The Hickses state we are the creators of our experiences, without exception. This leads to many questions that explain unwanted events in our lives like death, disease, accidents, loss of jobs, or lifetimes spent on unsuccessful pursuits. None of the LoA authors provide a clear answer to the question of why a person would be consciously or unconsciously sending out vibrations of harm, disease, or horrific events.

"You're telling me that I *asked* for all this?" Trisha said, so upset her voice shot up in volume and was shaking. Her eyes started to tear up. Her response stunned me because it came on so suddenly and with great emotion. Trisha and Jeremy lived next door, along with their three young children. My wife and I spent many afternoons and evenings with them for many years. We would share every detail of our lives, talking about jobs, kids, politics, and life.

That particular night, I was talking about a new concept I was learning about, the LoA. I went into great detail about how it came to be, who Esther and Jerry Hicks were, as well as Abraham, and how it was all supposed to work. Trisha and Jeremy were listening and asking questions, as usual, providing their perspectives and digging deeper into the concept. At one point in the conversation, I was explaining how the authors clearly stated all experiences that appear in our lives come to us through our emotional offerings to the Universe, without exception. In my description, I confidently applied the LoA concepts and spoke about finding the right car, job, or spouse. That was when Trisha exploded. A split-second later, we all knew exactly why she reacted so strongly and why it derailed that part of the discussion. A family member had emotionally and sexually abused Trisha for many years when she was a child. The trauma, as anyone would expect, had a devastating impact on her throughout her life.

"Ah, I don't ... I don't know what to say, Trisha. I'm sorry. I don't know what to say. I don't have any answers." I offered my lame reply, still reeling from the exchange.

"It's okay, Scott. No one can explain it; no one knows why." I think she saw my dismay and let me off the hook.

My guess is, if pressed on this situation, the authors of the LoA would answer by saying that everyone is on their own journey, and we cannot know why things happen to others or what reason or purpose unwanted events may hold. To be fair, no religion has a clear answer on how an omnipotent and loving God allows terrible things like what Trisha experienced to occur.

After gaining a good understanding of the LoA from the Hickses, I turned my attention back to Byrne's work in *The Secret*. Byrne states the secret is, in fact, the LoA, and describes similar core principles as in the Hicks, model. One significant contribution she offers traces the LoA concept through history. She provides examples of how it was used by the world's greatest minds like Plato, Shakespeare, Newton, Lincoln, and Einstein, among others.[2] A compelling component of her work is how she offers quotes and content from over twenty thought leaders in philosophy, physics, and literature, all sharing their success stories and support for the LoA concept.

Byrne also explains the LoA is a law of nature and is in effect at all times whether a person is aware of it or not, just as the Hickses present. She uses the same Hicks analogy of the radio tower, stating we are continually sending powerful signals of our thoughts out to the universe, and the content of our thoughts is subsequently manifested in our lives. Byrne also agrees with the Hickses in the idea of people not getting what they want because they focus their thoughts more on what they don't want than what they do want. Similar to the example of how a person fixated on *wanting* to be, do, or have something, will perpetuate the *wanting* experience rather than the experience of *having*.

According to Byrne, the same concept works if thoughts are focused on not *wanting* something. This is because the Universe does not recognize negative words like don't, not, or no. For example, if a person places their attention on *not wanting an unreliable car*, the Universe responds to the thought of *wanting* an unreliable car, leaving the *not* out, and will continue to provide the experience of an unreliable car.

I noticed an interesting correlation with this idea to something I learned when I was training to become a hypnotherapist. The theory was that the unconscious mind does not recognize negatives and perceives things as absolute values. An excellent example of how this translated to therapy was when a person needed help to stop smoking. We were taught not to focus on *stopping* smoking but instead to guide the client's visualizations to see themselves as a healthy and fit person. All references to stopping smoking, quitting smoking, or no longer smoking would be reinforcing *smoking*.

While emotions are critical in Byrne's process, as they are in the Hicks', she does not give as much attention to specific terminology to convey the various emotions. The most important emotions for Byrne are gratitude and thankfulness. As she states, "Gratitude is a powerful process for shifting your energy and bringing more of what you want into your life."[3] Also, she says that when you strongly feel as though you have what you are looking for, as if you already have it, you are believing that you have it and will, therefore, receive the object of your attention.

As with any theory, there are supporters and critics. One critic of the LoA is Neal Farber MD, Ph.D., a highly prolific writer on positive psychology, as well as a researcher on topics related to creating a positive work environment, mindfulness, goal-setting, productive communication, and positive parenting. In a 2014 article in *Psychology Today*, Farber provides an oversimplified and sarcastic review of the concept of the LoA and states that the success rate for those using the LoA is small, citing a statistic of 0.1% success rate.[4] He does not provide any references for this percentage.

In the article, Farber goes on to promote his theory, the "Principle of Attraction." His principle is a watered-down version of the LoA, stating that "like tends to attract like, positivity usually attracts positivity," and "negativity usually attracts negativity," centering around the idea of positive thinking.

It appears that Farber adhered to his principle of "negativity usually attracts negativity" by publishing a follow-up article in September of 2016 in *Psychology Today*, titled, "The Truth About the Law of Attraction."[5] In this article, he continues his obvious bias against LoA, listing fourteen reasons why the LoA does not exist. Farber's descriptions of the reasons are overwhelmingly critical and sarcastic to the point where, unfortunately, his credibility as a valid voice in the discussion is not useful. He ends his article, as with the first, with the unreferenced statistic of 0.1% success rate for the LoA, along with a plug for his newest book.

There are other critics of the LoA as well. For example, Jonathan Fields, a world-renowned author, business innovator, and producer and host of an internationally acclaimed podcast, the "Good Life Project," states the LoA is nothing mystical, spiritual, or quantum. It is basic human nature, and if anyone simply visualizes a desired outcome, they will adapt their behaviors to achieve that outcome.

Repeatedly visualizing a goal as if you had already attained it conditions you to believe it's possible. Over time, as that conditioning takes root through repetition, your belief in success leads you to act differently on many levels and take actions you'd never have taken.[6]

In addition, in my experience, psychologists critical of the LoA tend to discount other similar practices as well such as prayer, spiritual practices, belief in angels, and even religion in general. They categorize them as "magical thinking" and warn their patients about the dangers of beliefs not fully grounded in reality, or at least their version of it.

An advocate for the LoA concepts, Dr. Wayne Dyer, developed several books on the topic. However, he uses the term "Power of Intention" and offers a slightly different and broader perspective on this practice. The biggest mistake people make in approaching the LoA, according to Dyer, is they want and demand things. He goes on to state, "The law of attraction is this: You don't attract what you want. You attract what you are."[7]

In the Power of Intention material, Dyer states that in order to realize our desires, we must first align our thoughts and feelings with our inner selves. Then we act as if we already have what we desire. In this perspective, it is all about *allowing*, not *demanding*. Our action is more passive than directive, cultivated in an attitude of reverence for all life, sincerity, gentleness, and supportiveness.

Another popular author on the LoA is Gabby Bernstein, who offers an incredible array of books, YouTube videos, apps, and other resources on the topic, specifically about how to incorporate this idea into your life (gabbybernstein.com.) One exceptional book of the several she has authored is titled *Super Attractor* and presents the concept and provides examples of how it has worked for her. Gabby is a wonderful and passionate communicator with the ability to convey key themes of the LoA into simple statements like *Do less and attract more; Relax and trust that what you desire is on the way, know that spiritual guidance is available to you at all times and; Feel a sense of awe each day as you witness miracles unfold*. One unique perspective Gabby adds to the topic that no one else provides is an explanation of how spiritual guides are available to us all and how to start and maintain a connection with them.

To those of you who are interested in the idea of LoA and are wondering how it fits into the world of concrete logic, I would suggest you look up the YouTube video of an interview with Gabby and Tom Bilyeu, founder of Impact Theory. Tom's organization and mission is to give people the tools and knowledge they need to unlock their potential and impact the world. His pragmatic approach to addressing personal challenges appears to contradict the ideas contained in the LoA. The two engage in a wonderful discussion comparing and contrasting the two approaches. To find the video, search *Stop Needlessly Suffering Gabby Bernstein* on YouTube.

In terms of the four ways we can obtain knowledge about the LoA, there are many anecdotes and stories from people detailing how the LoA impacted their lives (authority). Also, many will hold fast to the idea that the LoA works or doesn't work (tenacity), and still others will have an innate understanding or acceptance of the idea (*a priori*). There will remain others who will want to see evidence and proof of the concept before accepting it as a viable theory (scientific observation).

LOA TAKEAWAYS

For me, the first takeaway is the LoA and intention are concepts worth spending time experimenting with and exploring. One reason for this is its simplicity. The fourteenth-century philosopher William Ockham proposed the idea that when considering several solutions to complicated issues, the simplest solution will be the most successful. This theory is called Ockham's Razor, or the Law of Parsimony, and is used in developing scientific theory. The simplicity of the LoA is that it states that what you project, you will receive. The statement "what goes around comes around" follows this idea, and I believe many of us have seen this play out in our lives and the lives of others.

A second takeaway is that the LoA provides an explanation of why there are 4,500 different religions around the world. These diverse belief systems work because their followers hold clear and consistent thoughts about expectations of their particular religion, experience something positive, and are committed to their faith. Whatever the person believes in, if their thoughts align with their beliefs and emotions, the LoA will provide.

A third takeaway is that the LoA could explain why many prayer studies don't work. If a person prays to be cured of an infection, the vibration will resonate with *infection*, and so it will persist. As in the large STEP bypass surgery prayer study, the people who were prayed for to have "no complications" had the most complications of the three study groups because the dominant vibration was *complications*.

A fourth takeaway is that the LoA could explain how hurtful and angry people are successful. The reason is they are aligned with their thoughts, energy, and emotions to create the experiences they want, even though it is not desirable from other people's perspectives.

An important note to remember is that the authors of the LoA and intention point out that these concepts are in place even if we are not consciously focused on them. Just as a sailboat will meander through the water if no one is controlling the rudder or sail, many people go through life the same way.

Getting back to the fundamental question, can we manifest things just by thinking about them? The answer is clear: it depends. What we are thinking about, what we want to see in our lives, how long have we been focused, and with what level of intensity, in addition to any underlying doubts, all come into play.

In any case, the concept of LoA, at least theoretically and intuitively, makes enough sense for me to consider and continue to experiment within different scenarios.

At the bare minimum, it encourages us to hold a positive attitude as we seek to be, do, or have things we would like to experience.

THREE EXPERIMENTS WITH THE LAW OF ATTRACTION

I was intrigued by the material offered on the topic of LoA, both in terms of the definitions and the many methods proposed in order to help people align their vibrations to obtain the things they wanted. So I decided to do some experiments on my own, with some interesting results. My sample size was one, and I was the lead investigator and participant. This does not fall into the category of good research design, but it was something.

I was working for a company that developed a medication adherence program to help people commit to taking their medications. Organizations that pay for the care of people, such as insurance companies, health systems, or employers, are interested in programs that will help keep their patients adherent to their medication schedule, and therefore healthy. However, any company that offered a program similar to ours faced a catch-22 situation. This was when the potential buyer might want to implement a program but wanted to see results from previous studies before committing. As a result, we needed a contract with someone willing to pay for a program with no evidence to support its success. That was my intention, my desire: a contract with one group or company to pilot our program.

Following the directions from the LoA materials, I took time each day to quiet my mind and visualize having a contract with an organization for our program. Many times, with meditative music playing in the background, I pictured a call coming through from one of our contacts who were excited to pilot the program, and I spent many hours visualizing precisely how we would introduce the program to the company's medical staff, human resource staff, and middle managers. I pictured myself and the situations completely, not only imagining the sights and sounds but also the smells and textures of the rooms where I would make these presentations. Some days I wasn't able to have a quiet moment, but overall, I was able to devote ten to fifteen mins a day for at least five days per week on the visualization process.

Weeks and months passed with us making presentations to dozens of companies and organizations. We always got the same response: "Come back when you have some data that shows this works." About six months after I began my regular visualization rituals, it happened. We were notified that a health system in Connecticut was willing to pilot the program with its three thousand employees. If the program produced positive results after six months, they would open it up to other groups.

This was our break. We were confident that if even one component of the program worked, and there were about a dozen, it would be considered a success and rolled out within a year or two to hundreds of thousands of people covered by the health system. I was ecstatic. It was an incredible project and opportunity, and we were all excited as we began to execute implementation plans and meetings to roll out the program.

This could be viewed as evidence the LoA worked. But maybe it was just our hard work that "manifested" the opportunity. Perhaps this was just a coincidence that randomly occurred by chance from the dozens of presentations we made. The fanatical supporters of LoA would make a big deal about these occurrences, claiming they were the results of the vibrations I offered. It was tough to tell and impossible to know for sure. But then something else happened.

About two weeks after we got the notification for the pilot, we were meeting with another health system. They informed us that they too wanted to pilot the program with their employees. They cited the same offer to expand to their hundreds of thousands of customers if the initial results were positive. With the odds against us landing any contracts with our untested program, now the second contract appeared on my desk. I couldn't help but wonder if this was further evidence of LoA. It still could have been the result of our efforts. But the results of random chance? Less likely. I concluded it might not be concrete proof but definitely was worth further consideration.

The second experiment I conducted was much shorter. My desire, this time, was winning the Powerball lottery. I applied the same process used in the medication adherence contracts as the lottery approached $400 million. For ten to fifteen minutes a day, with meditation music in the background, I visualized the things I would do if I won all that money in as much detail as possible. It all ended after about two weeks when someone in the Midwest won the money. I have no idea why it didn't work. Although I have always had doubts about how well I would handle being a multimillionaire.

The third experiment I conducted involved one of the loves of my life: motorcycles. And I applied the same meditation program for this experiment I used for in my other two, but this time it lasted ten months.

The study began in June of 2015 when I was at a motorcycle rally with some friends in Lake George, New York. It was a typical rally with thousands of motorcycle enthusiasts attending and participating in special events. Several motorcycle manufacturers were there as well, offering their latest models.

The bike I had then was a fifteen-year-old Honda Gold Wing, and even though I knew I couldn't afford it, I was interested in the new model. Gold Wings are large, expensive touring bikes specifically made for long rides. I went to the Honda booth to schedule a test drive of the new model the next morning.

As any motorcycle enthusiast has experienced, this ride was as close to love at first sight as one can get. I loved the power on the highway and the way it glided smoothly on the back roads. I was hooked. When I got back to the booth, I learned this was a new model, the F6B, and cost around $20,000. I had no idea how I would pay for it, but

I committed to myself that I would come back to the same rally the next year riding my new bike.

I quickly began the process of attraction I used for my other experiments. It was easy to visualize what I wanted, because I experienced it on the test drive. The big question was how to pay for it. Maybe my annual bonus, I thought, but in the past it had never been large enough to cover the cost of a new Gold Wing. When I had those thoughts, I reminded myself that doubts could short-circuit the positive vibrations of attraction. Otherwise, I would have been a millionaire by now by winning the lottery.

Months later, the riding season ended, and winter set in. I was regularly working on my desire with certainty, overriding my doubts, and believing that I would be riding my new bike in the spring. That December, I found a dealer near me that had it, and I asked about the price. My dream bike was going to cost me $22,000. Nevertheless, battling this new round of doubts that could ruin my vision, I told the sales guy I would be in to see it soon. December was also when we scheduled our year-end reviews at work. A year-end bonus would go a long way to help fund my dream because it was the only way I could get the cash infusion I needed.

I had my review, and it went well. My manager told me that the bonuses would be good since we had an exceptional year. She would let me know in the middle of March what the number would be. This was it. The stage was set. Spring was around the corner, the bike I wanted was sitting in a showroom about ten miles from my home, and a bonus was coming my way. I even booked the trip to the same rally where I first rode the same model the year before, and where I vowed to return this year on my new wheels.

When it came time for my manager to call me into her office to tell me about my bonus, I was dumbfounded. Unbelievable. The bonuses that year were higher than any other year in the company's history. The bonus I received was $22,000. It was the exact price of my dream bike — $22,000.

Does this prove the LoA? No. As any scientifically minded person will say, we can't prove anything. We can say this experiment supports the concept of the LoA mainly because several variables had to align for my vision to become a reality. I had no idea and no control over what my bonus would be. The fact that it matched the cost of my bike was remarkable.

Several weeks after I got the bike, my manager was walking by as I was parking my new two-wheeler at work. On the walk into the office, I briefly explained the concept of LoA and my experiment. Being an open-minded person, she seemed at least not to rule the idea out. I went further and asked if she happened to know somehow that I was looking for a new bike and got me the money I needed. She told me I was an idiot to think that she found out the type of bike I was looking for, did the research, selected a model, got an average price, and put in for that amount. Okay, I got it. It had been a ridiculous thing to ask her. But I had to ask.

In thinking about the LoA and whether it is a real and consistent phenomenon, it occurred to me this could be an alternative to what prayer is supposed to do. In this case, the focus is not a deity; the focus is becoming aware of our thoughts and emotions to create the outcomes we want. In the spirit of research, I emailed the Abraham-Hicks organization to ask if they would be interested in conducting a study to validate the LoA concepts. The organization replied that they do not get involved in any research relating to the LoA. They did not provide any other explanation or comment. The more I thought about it, I realized it would be harder to study the effects of LoA than prayer because of the subjectivity of the variables. Perhaps, too, they would not want the LoA to be disproven, the same reluctance prayer researchers wrestle with as well. Developing a set of questions that would quantify a person's emotional state that matched the LoA's twenty-two emotional descriptions, and detect changes, would be challenging to validate.

LESSON 12
WE ARE COCREATORS OF OUR REALITY

We see things not as they are, but as we are

One consistent question in my spiritual journey has been: to what degree can we influence, control, or navigate our world? I saw the evidence of how prayer and meditation could impact physical and mental conditions, but what about life situations the LoA claims to be able to accomplish? This is the difference between praying for good health and seeing health conditions improve versus wanting a specific car and then bumping into someone at the store and learning that one of their neighbors was moving and was selling the exact make and model.

From a religious perspective, the underlying mechanism of action in prayer is divine intervention. However, in the LoA, it is the Universe and the movement of energy that affects change. Assuming this is accurate, the next questions relate to how this might work. And are there any guiding principles to help explain these phenomena? After some searching, I was surprised to learn there is a discipline that sheds some light on these questions, as well as possible answers. This is the study of quantum physics, also known as quantum mechanics, or quantum theory.

The reason quantum physics is central in this exploration is that it provides a possible explanation of how our thoughts, prayers, and meditations might impact our world. Importantly, it reveals how the act of observing can change the world we see.

Before we delve into this topic, it is helpful to look at how we got to quantum physics from "regular" physics. As we all know from grade school, the study of physics started with Isaac Newton when he presented his laws of motion in the 1680s, stemming from the supposed apple falling on his head. Newton's work is identified as *classical physics* and centers on the movement of objects. His theories helped organize and predict the position and speed of objects in any timeframe in addition to accounting for the impact of gravity. From this perspective, the world is viewed as a series of mechanical objects with all movements and motions able to be predicted and manipulated. This thinking ignited the Scientific Revolution of the 1600s and the subsequent Industrial Revolution, which transformed the world through advances in the development of machinery, equipment, and productivity.

However, when scientists started looking more closely at how objects worked at the subatomic level, specifically at the behavior of atoms and their components, they found the physical world at this level did not operate exactly as Newton suggested in his classical theories.

Three findings challenged Newtonian theories at the subatomic levels and ushered in the discipline of quantum mechanics. One observation relates to the basic physical principle that when an object is heated, it emits light. The more heat applied, the more light is released. In studying this effect, the German physicist Max Planck was the first to discover that light was not emitted in smooth and continuously increasing energy waves when an object was heated. Albert Einstein confirmed this idea with his work on the Photoelectric Effect, showing that light is not a continual wave, but rather clumps of energy he called "photons." These acted as particles as they traveled through space.

Another example that contradicted classical physics is in the work of Danish physicist Niels Bohr in his studies of the hydrogen atom. This atom is simple because it has one electron orbiting around one proton. Bohr noted that, according to classical physics, the atom should be continually emitting radiation or light as the electron loses energy and collapses into the proton, but this was not how the electron behaved. What was happening was the electron emitted more or less energy depending on the size of its orbits and emitted no energy if it was in a stable orbit, opposite of what classical physics predicted.

Not too long after these discoveries were made, another aspect of light was revealed that shook the traditional ideas of physics to an even greater extent. The finding was made in the famous double-slit experiment, first conducted by Davisson and Germer in 1927. In this experiment, a beam of electrons was shown through a board containing two vertical slits and projected on a screen. The classical physics model predicted the light on the screen would be concentrated directly opposite each of the slits, showing just two lines of light on the screen. However, what appeared was a series of several bright and dark bands. The explanation for this was the light coming through the slits did not move in a straight line as particles, but instead changed to behave as waves that either joined or canceled waves from the neighboring slit. This produced several bands of light on the screen, just like two intersecting ripples in a pond. The results of these experiments, in addition to Einstein's Photoelectric Effect and Plank's work in blackbody radiation, revealed that light could act as a wave and a particle depending on the environment.

Even more interesting was what happened when scientists attempted to observe precisely when the shift from particle to wave occurred as the electrons passed through the slits. As mentioned, when the stream of electrons passed through the slits, they changed from particles to waves. But when exactly did this change happen? To answer this question, scientists set up observation points before, after, and at the slits to see when the shift occurred. The results showed that at whatever point the electrons were observed, they would act as particles. When they weren't observed while passing through the slits, they would transition to waves. This means that even after the electrons passed through the slits and were acting like waves, once observation began, they would revert to particle behavior. In scientific terms, the act of observation caused the collapse of the wave function. These discoveries led German physicist Werner Heisenberg to present the principle called the Observation Effect, suggesting we can change the behavior of physical systems through observation. To be clear, the observation mentioned in these studies related to the physical apparatus used to monitor the flow of the electrons, not the conscious observation of humans.

Quantum theory takes us to a different place when considering how we interact with the world around us. There are four insights from the quantum shift worth noting.

OBSERVATION CAN CHANGE THINGS

When considering the impact of observation, we can separate the topic into three broad categories: physical, mental, and behavioral. While the Observation Effect in physics showed how the behavior of light is impacted by physical observation, there is some evidence showing that mental observation can produce change as well. The category of research is called Mind-Matter Interaction, with studies conducted in this field since the 1800s. The two subjects studied most often involve dice-tossing and random number generators (RNG). These are electrical circuits that output random bits of data of either a 1 or a 0.

In dice studies, researchers conducted an analysis of many studies to determine if there was evidence of mental intentions influencing the outcome of tossed dice. They reviewed outcomes of seventy-three published studies where the participants attempted to mentally influence the dice for a specific face number to appear face up. The review revealed a total of 2,569 participants had attempted to mentally influence 2.6 million dice throws in 148 separate experiments with fifty-two investigators. Forty-four percent of the 148 studies reported significant findings. In other words, statistically speaking, people's thoughts did influence the dice.[1]

RNGs can be considered an electronic version of dice studies. These studies focused on the mental influence of an electronic circuit that produces a stream of approximately 1,000 random 1s or 0s per second. This means the chance of the circuit producing either a 1 or 0 is 50%. In a similar approach to the dice studies, participants in these studies attempted to mentally influence what value appeared, a 1 or 0. Researchers identified 832 studies conducted by sixty-eight different investigators. Of these studies, 258 were part of an investigation conducted by Princeton University's Princeton Engineering Anomalies Research (PEAR) laboratory.[2] The results showed an overall effect of 50.9%, a .9 % shift from chance. While this appears to be a relatively small shift, the results show that, statistically, people's thoughts did influence the electronic device.

Other evidence of the impact of mental interactions with our bodies can be seen in studies of biofeedback and, as mentioned earlier, meditation, as well as the placebo effect. In summary, there is a good case to say that, at least to some degree, we can influence the physical world through our mental observations.

The last category of observation is behavioral. An example comes from social psychology with the Hawthorne Effect. Henry Landsberger developed the term in 1958 as he reviewed the results of productivity studies at the Hawthorne Works factory of General Electric near Chicago, Illinois.[3] The factory management wanted to explore ways to improve productivity, and they started by observing lighting conditions. Their studies showed that workers increased productivity as the brightness in the room increased. Wanting to learn more, they conducted additional studies and found that productivity also increased when changes in workstations were made and break times were adjusted. Landsberger made two other observations that caused him to question the impact of the workplace changes on their ultimate productivity. One was that productivity decreased after the study concluded, and second, sometimes productivity increased even when the workplace changes reverted to the original setting. He concluded that the workers worked harder because they knew they were being observed. In other words, whatever reason the workers changed their behavior (e.g. fear of being fired, wanting to do better than others, etc.), Landsberger's action of conducting the study impacted productivity.

OUR PERCEPTION OF OUR WORLD IS INCOMPLETE

Drs. Deepak Chopra and Menas Kafatos, in their book *You Are the Universe*,[4] propose that our brains are limited in their ability to record all aspects of our surroundings. For example, visible light represents only .01% of the electromagnetic spectrum. This means that our eyes are not able to see the bulk of all the frequencies that engulf us in the form of gamma rays, radio waves, X-rays, and microwaves. The authors also point out that there is no light inside our skulls. Our cranium only contains our brain, which assembles signals from our eyes and optical network to create the experience of light. Our brains organize information from all sensory inputs (sight, taste, touch, hearing, and smell) to create our experiences. This means we are always one step removed from reality. Just as a picture or video of an ocean is not the ocean, but rather an image processed through camera sensors, our perception is not reality, but instead a combination of sensory inputs used to create what we perceive as reality.

WE ARE INTERCONNECTED WITH THE WORLD WE PERCEIVE

Nobel Prize laureate and physicist Niels Bohr expands on the concept of the impact of observation, stating that we can never have total knowledge of the world because as we observe something, we change the thing we are observing. According to Bohr, quantum physics can only make predictions and observations but cannot explain anything about the world we assume to exist outside of our observations.

Bohr provides a startling insight that any event we experience and observe must be seen as an interconnected totality, meaning that the observer and the object are interacting with each other.[5] Einstein's theories support this idea by showing that matter is another form of energy. This suggests that reality is an interaction of physical material and energy.[6] In other words, as stated by Drs. Chopra and Kafatos, "We project ourselves into everything we experience, not just by observing, but by participating in the reality that emerges." [7]

WE DON'T KNOW WHAT WE DON'T KNOW

Some people question the ideas of the LoA, observation effect, or an interconnected reality, saying they are unscientific. While it is always good to apply some level of skepticism to new ideas, we have to remember that science is only our latest best guess of how our world works. We hear about significant discoveries every year that take us far beyond anyone ever thought possible. In reality, we have a long way to go to understand many things, and some relate to the most fundamental components of our world. As Dr. Caleb Scharf, director of astrobiology at Columbia University,[8] points out, we don't know what dark energy is, and it comprises over 68% of our universe. Also, we are just starting to understand the quantum nature of reality, black holes, the possibility of multiverses, and quantum firewalls. Other areas where we lack understanding are the composition and movements of material deep within the Earth's core and why we can't live without microbial cells in our bodies. We don't even exactly know how photosynthesis works or how it has provided life-giving oxygen to our planet for millennia. The list goes on and on. The point here is that just because we do not understand a new concept or theory, it doesn't mean it does not exist. Many times, science follows the pursuit of real phenomena.

QUANTUM TAKEAWAY

Quantum physics is a complicated topic, and an in-depth discussion is certainly beyond the scope of this book. Nevertheless, the basic principles described here suggest that reality, from our point of view, could be shifting right before our eyes. Reality is not reality. Also, I suggest that the LoA could be the mechanism of how matter and energy interact to create the world we experience. In other words, these quantum insights propose that as we move through our lives, what we see and experience is a fraction of what is really happening around us and may be changing as we go, influenced by our emotions, thoughts, and intentions.

To what extent we can change our world and how fast are the critical questions. Does this mean that if I want a used Boeing 747, one will appear in my backyard? Ridiculous. However, if we're looking for specific things or situations and hold consistent thoughts about them, forces that we do not know about now will possibly align the opportunities, connections, and coincidences to bring those experiences into our lives.

If so, this is a true paradigm shift in how we view ourselves in relation to the world around us and speaks to the heart of what I would like to convey in these pages.

SUMMARY

Interpreting what we are seeing and experiencing at any given moment can be accomplished on a few different levels. On one level, we can see what is physically happening and interpret the situation. In this case, it is a matter of spinning it to be positive, negative, or neutral. On another level, we can acknowledge we are interconnected with what is happening and influencing it in some way. This is what the LoA suggests. Quantum theory provides rationale that may support this idea, stating that we are interconnected with the physical world and can influence it through observation. The final point is that there is much about the universe that we do not know. We do not know much about the different types of energy, or how they interact with each other, and we certainly do not understand how we interact with them.

I suggest you conduct experiments in your own life and see what happens. It's an exciting proposition. Are you up for it?

DISCUSSION QUESTIONS

- Do you believe you can influence the path of your life in any way, whether through prayer, meditation, the Law of Attraction, or just thinking or wishing? If so, what has been successful for you?

- Have you experienced anything like the Law of Attraction suggests? Did something happen that would be hard to say it was a coincidence?

- Did the discussion on quantum physics impact your thinking? If so, how?

- Does the idea that we are cocreators of our lives make you feel uncomfortable? If so, why?

NOTES

NOTES

ON BEING ANGELS

As I mentioned at the beginning of this book, I will say again that if you are satisfied with your current beliefs, religion, or practices, *please* do not make any changes. Just because organized religion did not work for me does not mean it cannot work for you.

The most profound change I experienced as a result of my journey was the shift in perception of seeing myself as part of God, a messenger, an angel. I finally understood that God was not "out there" somewhere. As a result, for the first time in my life, I felt unconditionally accepted and connected to everyone and everything. The immense freedom I felt moving from my fear-based religious background altered my life forever. I was enlightened.

In accepting and experiencing our divine nature, there are three areas I believe are the most important to keep in mind.

WE ARE ETERNAL

This is not a foreign concept to religion. Several of the world's faiths believe that our souls transition from this body to another place. It is what happens during and after that journey that differs. From a path to judgment, as in the New Testament, or the forty-nine-day transition process as in the *Tibetan Book* of the Dead, or Neale Donald Walsch's detailed description found in his book, *Home with God: In a life that Never Ends*.[1] There is no way to verify what anyone claims actually happens, but Walsch's is a fascinating depiction of a journey I highly recommend reading.

One aspect of the idea of eternal life that has impacted me is mentioned several times throughout the work of the Hickses. It is the idea that because we are eternal beings, there is no destination. Our journey spans hundreds of lifetimes. We will never get "it" done, whatever "it" is; we will never arrive at a final destination. The reason we will never accomplish everything we want is that we will continually seek new challenges, lifetime after lifetime. This means it is all about the journey. The focus is on exploring our interests, concentrating on being true to ourselves and not worrying about a timeline.

WE ARE CONNECTED

Understanding that we are angels means that we are connected in two aspects. First, we are connected to God, the Universe, Spirit, a higher consciousness, or whatever you want to call it; there is no separation. So, what does this mean exactly? Technically, it means that our bodies are extensions of some sort of a nonphysical world. Most of us are not tuned in to the spiritual world all the time; our attention is focused on our physical lives, work, school, and relationships. Religious and spiritual practices and meditation provide ways to connect with Spirit that promote the experience and feeling of being a part of something bigger than ourselves.

Neurologists at the University of Pennsylvania Medical School, Drs d'Aquilli and Newburg, conducted some fascinating research around our brains' feelings of oneness and spiritual experiences. In their work, they explain that the area of the brain that is responsible for providing us with a sense of our orientation in space and time is the parietal lobe. To test this idea, they scanned the brains of experienced Tibetan Buddhist meditators with a single-photon emission computed tomography (SPECT) scanner. They discovered there was less activity in the parietal lobe area. The researchers hypothesized that the act of meditation blocked sensory and cognitive input into this area, providing a sense of timelessness and limitless space. To further confirm their ideas, they conducted experiments with the same scanner on people as they meditated. Interestingly, the results showed increased activity in the frontal lobe, indicating increased attention and concentration, which occurs in meditation. As hypothesized, the results showed a decrease of activity in the parietal lobe during meditation.[2]

I bring this research up not to explain away God or Spirit but to present how our brains create mystical experiences of oneness. For me, a larger question is why do we even have a parietal lobe? Could it be so that we would have the ability to experience separation and all the highs and lows of life that come with that? Could it be the only way we, as eternal beings, can have a temporary physical existence? Maybe.

The second way we are connected is with everyone. Certainly, our bodies are separate from other physical things, and most times, our minds are. I think most would agree that our minds can sometimes interact with others in situations when we have been thinking about someone right before they call us. Or when two people are so in sync that they finish each other's sentences and seemingly know what the other is thinking. A framework of how this works was proposed by Carl Jung in his idea of the Collective Consciousness. This is the idea that all people have a shared connection deep within the unconscious mind. Interestingly, in a recent article on Integrated Information Theory (IIT), mathematician/physicist Dr. Johannes Kleiner at the Munich Centre for Mathematical Philosophy in Germany suggests that the ITT supports the idea that the universe is conscious. If so, "This could be the beginning of a scientific revolution," says Dr. Kleiner.[3]

The implication of this idea is that we all are connected by some common energy. Some suggest that the common energy is God, or life, or love. Nothing else in the universe exists outside of this. We experience a lack of love, God, or life if we choose to pinch ourselves off of this source energy by harboring feelings of anger, hatred, and negativity. In a sense, there is no such thing as evil; it's a lack of love. Negativity has no energy in itself.

Who knows if some type of energy connects us, but one thing we all can agree on is that everyone on this planet is connected as human beings. A powerful realization is that we are all brothers and sisters. This means that if we launch a missile at another group of people, we are actually killing ourselves. Sadly, this concept is not prevalent on our planet. Maybe someday it will be, in the meantime, I boldly stand with a minority that believes we are all family.

WE ARE CAPABLE

Possibly the most significant deterrent to embracing our divine nature is that we hold on to limiting beliefs. These beliefs are embedded in our minds, just under the surface. We all know what they are; they generate messages to let us know we are not good enough, smart enough, or good-looking, or funny, or a good parent, and on, and on, and on. Sometimes we are aware of them, other times they are in the background. We look at them like at the sun; a quick glance, then look away. These are painful beliefs triggered by us when we compare ourselves with others or are embedded by others over time, telling us we are not good enough.

As we learn to embrace our divine nature, we will sense that, at our core, we are pure, pristine, and connected to all the powers of the Universe, as any angel would understand. Gone are the doubts of worthiness, because sin is no longer an issue, and over time, our limiting beliefs will fade. We are enough.

But what about our capabilities? We can be enough, but we do not have superpowers, we don't have wings and halos — well at least I do not. But we do have some abilities, and many of us can say that we have accomplished a few things, or we have helped someone in a profound way. I'm sure you have heard stories of people achieving extraordinary feats that challenge our understanding of the physical limits of our world. Sometimes we see them in action in situations of great need, sometimes in quiet places of solitude. Whatever the case, if we look, we can see them all around us. And if we are courageous, we will realize we are capable beyond our own [limiting] beliefs.

In this book I presented my journey and how we can all learn to embrace our divine and eternal nature. In the next book, *Angel in Training: Calling all Angels!* I will review what ancient traditions and culture have been saying about them for centuries. I will also describe what the current physical sciences say about these entities and how they can possibly interact with our world. A psychological perspective of the topic will be shown, with some interesting conclusions. Most importantly, I would like to include personal experiences and stories of people who have experienced angels in their lives or in their own behavior.

If you have been involved with a situation where you witnessed an angel in action and would like to share your experiences, please send an email to scott@angelintraining.org.

Thank you for being a part of the *Angel in Training* community!

SCOTT GUERIN

COMING SOON!
ANGEL IN TRAINING – CALLING ALL ANGELS!

From all the information we have on angels, they can be bright white with wings, or they can appear as ordinary people. They can be strong and fast, and they can be warriors. But is that all we know?

This book continues our divine journey exploring three fundamental areas in gaining an understanding of angels. The first is discovering what the world's great religions have had to say about the origins of angels and their role in humanity. The second is to review what the physical sciences currently say about these entities and how they can interact with our world. This section will also include a fascinating psychological review of the subject from the perspective of the emotion, perception, and disfunction.

Most importantly, I would like to include current stories from people who have experienced angelic or divine intervention. If you have a story that you would like to share where something positive and wonderful happened, please send it in to me. The purpose of this is to provide examples of hope and courage for people in both good times and in times of need.

Please send an email to scott@angelintraining.org

Thank you for being a part of the
Angel in Training community!

SUGGESTED READINGS

Arntz, William and Matthew Hoffman, Betty Chasse, and Mark Vincente. *What the Bleep Do We Know?* Captured Light and Lord of the Winds Films, LLC, 2004.

Bernstein, Gabrielle. *Super Attractor: Methods for Manifesting a Life beyond Your Wildest Dreams.* Carlsbad, CA: Hay House, Inc., 2019.

Byrne, Rhonda. *The Secret.* Atria Books/Beyond Words. 2006.

Campbell, Joseph and Moyers, William. *Joseph Campbell and the Power of Myth with Bill Moyers.* Audio CD. Maryland: Highbridge Company, 2001.

Chopra, Deepak and Kafatos, Menas. *You are the Universe.* New York: Harmony Books, 2017.

Dyer, Wayne. *Wisdom of the Ages.* Boston: HarperCollins, 2002.

Hahn, Thich Nhat. *Living Buddha, Living Christ.* New York: Riverhead Books, 1995.

Hicks, Esther and Hicks, Jerry. *Ask, and It Is Given.* Carlsbad, California, Hay House, Inc., 2004.

Kanigel, Robert. *The Man Who Knew Infinity: A Life of the Genius, Ramanujan.* New York: C. Scribner's, 1991.

Myss, Caroline. *Anatomy of the Spirit.* New York: Harmony Books, 1996.

Newton, Michael. *Journey of Souls.* St. Paul, Minnesota: Llewellyn Publications, 1988.

Reiss, Steven. *The 16 Strivings for God.* Macon, Georgia: Mercer University Press, 2015.

Stevenson, Ian. *20 Cases in Support of Reincarnation (2nd ed)*. Charlottesville, VA: University Press of Virginia, 1974.

Thetford, William T. and Schucman, Helen. *A Course in Miracles*. Mill Valley, CA: Foundation of Inner Peace, 1975.

Walsch, Neale Donald. The Conversations with God Series.

Wattles, Wallace D. *The Science of Getting Rich*. Langhorn, Pennsylvania, JonRose Publishing, 1910.

Weiss, Brian. *Many Lives, Many Masters*. New York: Simon & Schuster, 1988.

REFERENCES

LESSON 1 — WE CREATE OUR PERCEPTIONS ABOUT GOD

1. Lukoff, David, Robert Turner, and Lu Francis. "Transpersonal Psychology Research Review: Psychoreligious Dimensions of Healing." *The Journal of Transpersonal Psychology* 24, no.1 (1992): 41–60.

2. Bronfenbrenner, Urie. *The Ecology of Human Development*. Cambridge, MA: Harvard University Press, 1979.

3. Fowler, James, W. *Stages of Faith: The psychology of human development and the quest for meaning*. San Francisco, CA: Harper and Row, 1981.

LESSON 2 — RELIGION AND SPIRITUALITY ARE TWO DISTINCT CONCEPTS

1. Schneiders, Sandra. "Spirituality in the Academy," Theological Studies 50 (1989): 684.

2. Decker, Larry. "The Role of Trauma in Spiritual Development." *Journal of Humanistic Psychology* 33, no. 4 (1993): 33–46; Meraviglia, Marha G. "Critical Analysis of Spirituality and its Empirical Indicators." *Journal of Holistic Nursing* 17, no.1 (March 1999): 18–34.

LESSON 3 — THERE ARE MANY WAYS TO GOD

1. Hahn, Thich Nhat. *Living Buddha, Living Christ*. New York: Riverhead Books, 1995.

2. Stevenson, Ian. *20 Cases in Support of Reincarnation (2nd ed)*. Charlottesville, VA: University Press of Virginia, 1974.

3. Weiss, Brian. *Many Lives, Many Masters*. New York: Simon & Schuster, 1988.

4. Newton, Michael. *Journey of Souls*. St. Paul, Minnesota: Llewellyn Publications, 1988.

5. Reiss, Steven. *The 16 Strivings for God*. Macon, Georgia: Mercer University Press, 2015.

LESSON 4 — RESOLVING CONFLICTING BELIEFS

1. Baron, Robert and Dean Byrne. *Social Psychology (8th ed.)* Needham Heights: Allyn & Bacon, 1997.

LESSON 5 — WHO DECIDES WHAT IS TRUE?

1. Pierce, Charles S. "The Fixation of Belief." *Popular Science Monthly* 12, (November 1887): 1-15. http://www.peirce.org/writings/p107.html.

PRAYER: A LIFELINE?

1. Keefe, Frances J., James Crisson, Bruno J. Urban, and David Williams. "Analyzing chronic low back pain: The relative contribution of pain coping strategies." *Pain* 40, no. 3 (March 1990): 203-301.

2. Byrd, Randolph. "Positive therapeutic effects of intercessory prayer in a coronary care unit population." *Southern Medical Journal* 81, no. 7 (July 1988): 826-829.

3. Carroll, S. "Spirituality and purpose in life in alcoholism recovery." *Journal of Studies on Alcohol* 54, no. 3 (1993): 297-301.

4. Levin, J.S., J.S. Lyons, and D.B. Larson. "Prayer and health during pregnancy: Findings from the Galveston Low Birthweight Survey." *Southern Medical Journal* 86, no. 9 (1993): 1022-1027.

5. Collipp, P.J. "The efficacy of prayer: A triple-blind study." *Medical Times* 97, no. 5 (1969): 201-204.

6. 2 Samuel 12: 16-23.

7. McCullough, M. "Prayer and Health: Conceptual issues, research review, and research agenda." *Journal of Psychology and Theology* 23, No. 1 (1995): 16.

8. Ibid.

9. Simão, Talita P., Silvia Caldeira, and Emilia C. De Carvalho. "The Effect of Prayer on Patients' Health: Systematic Literature Review." *Religions* 7, no. 1 (2016): 11.

DOES PRAYING FOR OTHERS WORK?

1. Galton, Francis. "Statistical studies into the efficacy of prayer." *Fortnightly Review* 12, (1872): 125–135.

2. Joyce, C. Richard and R.M.C. Weldon. "The Objective Efficacy of Prayer: A double-blind clinical trial." *The Journal of Chronic Diseases* 18, (1965): 367–377. https://doi.org/10.1016/0021-9681(65)90040-8.

3. Collipp, P.J. "The efficacy of prayer: A triple-blind study." *Medical Times* 97, no. 5 (1969): 201–204.

4. Byrd, Randolph. "Positive therapeutic effects of intercessory prayer in a coronary care unit population." *Southern Medical Journal* 81, no. 7 (July 1988): 826–829.

5. Byrd, "Positive therapeutic effects," 827.

6. Byrd, "Positive therapeutic effects," 829.

7. Harris, William S., et al. "A Randomized, Controlled Trial of the Effects of Remote, Intercessory Prayer on Outcomes in Patients Admitted to the Coronary care unit." *Archives of Internal Medicine* 159, no.19 (1999): 2273–2278.

8. Sicher, F., E. Targ, D. Moore, and H. Smith "A randomized, double-blind study of the effect of distant healing in a population with advanced AIDS: Report of a small scale study." *Western Journal of Medicine* 169, no. 6 (1998): 356–363.

9. Benson, H., J.A. Dusek, J.B. Sherwood, P. Lam, C.F. Bethea, W. Carpenter, S. Levitsky, P.C. Hill, D.W. Clem Jr., M.K. Jain, D. Dumel, S.L. Kopecky, P.S. Muller, D. Marek, S. Rollins, P.L. Hibberd. "Study of the therapeutic effects of intercessory prayer (STEP) in cardiac bypass patients — A multi-center randomized trial of uncertainty and certainty of receiving intercessory prayer." *American Heart Journal* 151, no. 4 (April 2006): 934–42.

10. Guerin, Scott. "The Effects on Quality of Life on Those who Pray and Meditate for Others." *The International Journal of Healing and Caring*. (Sept 2009). https://www.ijhc.org/the-effects-on-quality-of-life-on-those-who-pray-and-meditate-for-others-scott-guerin.

LESSON 6 — MEDITATION IS AN EFFECTIVE WAY TO EXPERIENCE PEACE AND THE PRESENCE OF GOD

1. Benson, Herbert. *Four Decades of Mind Body and Spirituality Findings*. Presented at Spirituality & Healing in Medicine. Boston, MA, Dec 1–2, 2007.

LESSON 7 — GOD IS STILL COMMUNICATING

1. Walsch, Neale Donald. *Conversations with God: an uncommon dialogue, Book 1*. New York: G.P. Putnam's Son's, 2002.

2. Walsch, Neale Donald. *The New Revelations: A Conversation with God*. New York: Atria Books, 2002.

3. Walsch, *The New Revelations*, 3.

4. Walsch, *The New Revelations*, 98.

5. Walsch, *The New Revelations*, 9.

LESSON 8 — THERE IS NO SEPARATION BETWEEN GOD AND US

1. Thetford, William T, and Helen Schucman. *A Course in*

Miracles. Mill Valley, CA: Foundation of Inner Peace, 1975.

2. Thetford and Schucman, *A Course in Miracles*, 8.

3. Thetford and Schucman, *A Course in Miracles*, 10.

4. Thetford and Schucman, *A Course in Miracles*, 11.

5. Thetford and Schucman, *A Course in Miracles*, 25.

6. Dyer, Wayne. *Wisdom of the ages*. Boston: HarperCollins, 2002.

LESSON 9 — VALIDATING BELIEF SYSTEMS

1. Roberts, Jane. *The Seth Material*. Manhasset, New York: New Awareness Network, Inc., 1970.

2. Flournoy, Theodore. *From India to the Planet Mars: A study of a case of somnambulism*. trans. Daniel B. Vermilye. New York: Harper & Brothers Publishers, 1901.

3. Albert Einstein Site. "Albert Einstein Quotes — Science." Accessed May 15, 2019. http://www.alberteinsteinsite.com/quotes /einsteinquotes.html#religon.

4. Kanigel, Robert. *The man who knew infinity: a life of the genius, Ramanujan*. New York: C. Scribner's, 1991.

5. Kanigel, *The man who knew infinity*, 281.

6. Kanigel, *The man who knew infinity*, 7.

LESSON 11 — THE LAW OF ATTRACTION

1. Wattles, Wallace D. *The Science of Getting Rich*. Langhorn, Pennsylvania: JonRose Publishing, 1910, 9.

2. Wattles, *The Science of Getting Rich*, 17.

3. Wattles, *The Science of Getting Rich*, 65.

4. Hicks, Esther and Jerry Hicks. *Ask, and it is Given*. Carlsbad, CA: Hay House, Inc., 2004, xxi.

5. Hicks, *Ask, and it is Given*, 25.

HOW THE LAW OF ATTRACTION WORKS

1. Hicks, Esther and Jerry Hicks. *Ask, and it is Given.* Carlsbad, CA: Hay House, Inc., 2004, 114.

2. Byrne, Rhonda. *The Secret.* Atria Books/Beyond Words, 2006, ix.

3. Byrne, *The Secret*, 93.

4. Farber, Neil. "The Law of Attraction Revisited." Accessed January 18, 2018. https://www.psychologytoday.com/blog/the-blame-game/201401/the-law-attraction-revisited.

5. Farber, Neil. "The Truth about the Law of Attraction." Accessed January 20, 2018. https://www.psychologytoday.com/blog/the-blame-game/201609/the-truth-about-the-law-attraction.

6. Fields, Jonathan. "I've got a Secret: The Law of Attraction is a lie." Accessed May 20, 2020. https://www.jonathanfields.com/ive-got-a-secret-the-law-of-attraction-is-a-lie/.

7. Dyer, Wayne. "The Power of Intention." Accessed July 20, 2019. https://www.drwaynedyer.com/press/power-intention/.

LESSON 12 — WE ARE COCREATORS OF OUR REALITY

1. Radin, Dean and Diane Ferrari. "Effects of consciousness on the fall of dice: A meta-analysis." *Journal of Scientific Exploration* 5 (1991): 61–84.

2. Jahn, Robert, et. al. "Correlations of random binary sequences with pre-stated operator intention: A review of a 12-year program." *Journal of Scientific Exploration* 11, no. 3 (1997): 345–367.

3. Roethlisberger, F.J. and William J. Dickson. *Volume V Management and the worker*, ed. Kenneth Thompson,

London: Routledge, 2003.

4. Chopra, Deepak and Menas Kafatos. *You Are the Universe*. New York: Harmony Books, 2017, 148.

5. Battista, John R. "Abraham Maslow, and Roberto Assagioli: Pioneers of Transpersonal Psychology." In *Textbook of Transpersonal Psychiatry and Psychology*, ed. Scotton, Bruce, Allen B. Chinen, and John R. Battista. New York: BasicBooks, 1996, 52–61.

6. Wade, Jenny. *Changes of Mind*. Albany: State University of New York Press, 1996.

7. Chopra, Deepak and Menas Kafatos. *You Are the Universe*, 148.

8. Scharf, Caleb. "This Is What We Don't Know About The Universe." Accessed February 3, 2019. https://blogs.scientificamerican.com/life-unbounded/this-is-what-we-done28099t-know-about-the-universe/.

ON BEING ANGELS

1. Walsch, Neale Donald. *Home with God: In a Life that Never ends*. New York, NY: Atria Books, 2006.

2. Newberg, Andrew. "Research Questions." Accessed April 25, 2020. http://www.andrewnewberg.com/research.

3. Brooks, Michael. "Is the universe conscious?" https://www.newscientist.com/article/mg24632800-900-is-the-universe-conscious-it-seems-impossible-until-you-do-the-maths/#ixzz6L77c91Ip.

www.ingramcontent.com/pod-product-compliance
Lightning Source LLC
Chambersburg PA
CBHW051359290426
44108CB00015B/2077